Microsoft® Excel 2002
Illustrated Basic

Elizabeth Eisner Reding
Lynn Wermers

COURSE
TECHNOLOGY
™
THOMSON LEARNING

Australia • Canada • Mexico • Singapore • Spain • United Kingdom • United States

COURSE TECHNOLOGY
™
THOMSON LEARNING

Microsoft Excel 2002 - Illustrated Basic

Elizabeth Eisner Reding
Lynn Wermers

Managing Editor:
Nicole Jones Pinard

Product Manager:
Emily Heberlein

Associate Product Manager:
Emeline Elliott

Production Editor:
Karen Jacot

Developmental Editor:
Barbara Clemens

Editorial Assistant:
Christina Kling Garrett

QA Manuscript Reviewers:
John Freitas, Ashlee Welz, Alex White, Harris Bierhoff, Serge Palladino, Holly Schabowski, Jeff Schwartz

Text Designer:
Joseph Lee, Black Fish Design

Composition House:
GEX Publishing Services

Disclaimer
Course Technology reserves the right to revise this publication and make changes from time to time in its content without notice.

Trademarks
Some of the product names and company names used in this book have been used for identification purposes only and may be trademarks or registered trademarks of their respective manufacturers and sellers.

Microsoft and the Office logo are either registered tradmarks or trademarks of Microsoft Corporation in the Unites States and/or other countries. Course Technology is an independent entity from Microsoft Corporation, and not affiliated with Microsoft in any manner.

This text may be used in assisting students to prepare for a Microsoft Office User Specialist Exam. Neither Microsoft Corporation, its designated review company, nor Course Technology warrants that use of this text will ensure passing the relevant exam.

Use of the Microsoft Office User Specialist Approved Courseware Logo on this product signifies that it has been independently reviewed and approved in complying with the following standards: "When used in conjunction with *Microsoft Excel – Illustrated Intermediate*, includes acceptable coverage of all content related to the Microsoft Office Exam entitled Microsoft Excel 2002 Core, and sufficient performance-based exercises that relate closely to all required content, based on sampling of text."

"When used in conjunction with *Microsoft Excel – Illustrated Intermediate* and *Microsoft Excel – Illustrated Advanced*, includes acceptable coverage of all content related to the Microsoft Office Exams entitled Microsoft Excel 2002 Core and Microsoft Excel 2002 Expert, and sufficient performance-based exercises that relate closely to all required content, based on sampling of text."

ISBN 0-619-04530-2

The Illustrated Series Vision

Teaching and writing about computer applications can be extremely rewarding and challenging. How do we engage students and keep their interest? How do we teach them skills that they can easily apply on the job? As we set out to write this book, our goals were to develop a textbook that:

▶ works for a beginning student

▶ provides varied, flexible and meaningful exercises and projects to reinforce the skills

▶ serves as a reference tool

▶ makes your job as an educator easier, by providing resources above and beyond the textbook to help you teach your course, including **Annotated Instructor's Editions** (in .pdf format) and suggested **Course Outlines**

Our popular, streamlined format is based on advice from instructional designers and customers. This flexible design presents each lesson on a two-page spread, with step-by-step instructions on the left, and screen illustrations on the right. This signature style, coupled with high-caliber content, provides a comprehensive yet manageable introduction to Microsoft Excel 2002—it is a teaching package for the instructor and a learning experience for the student.

AUTHORS ACKNOWLEDGMENTS

Elizabeth Eisner Reding: Creating a book of this magnitude is a team effort: I would like to thank my husband, Michael, for putting up with my ridiculous mood swings, Emily Heberlein, the project manager, and my development editor, Barbara Clemens, for her insightful suggestions and corrections. I would also like to thank the production and editorial staff for all their hard work that made this project a reality.

Lynn Wermers: Thanks to my editor, Barbara Clemens, for her helpful suggestions and encouragement.

Thanks also to the reviewers who provided invaluable feedback and ideas to us: Judy Irvine and Glenn Rogers (Western Nevada Community College).

Preface

Each 2-page spread focuses on a single skill.

Concise text that introduces the basic principles in the lesson and integrates the brief case study (indicated by the paintbrush icon).

Excel 2002

Changing Attributes and Alignment

Attributes are styling formats such as bold, italics, and underlining that you can apply to affect the way text and numbers look in a worksheet. You can also change the alignment of labels and values in cells to be left, right, or center. You can apply attributes and alignment options from the Formatting toolbar or from the Alignment tab of the Format Cells dialog box. See Table C-2 for a list and description of the available attribute and alignment toolbar buttons. ✎ Now that you have applied new fonts and font sizes to his worksheet labels, Jim wants you to further enhance the worksheet's appearance by adding bold and underline formatting and centering some of the labels.

Steps

1. Press **[Ctrl][Home]** to move to cell A1, then click the **Bold button** 🅱 on the Formatting toolbar
The title appears in bold.

2. Select the range **A3:J3**, then click the **Underline button** 🅤 on the Formatting toolbar
Excel underlines the text in the column headings in the selected range.

QuickTip
Overuse of any attribute can be distracting and make a workbook less readable. Be consistent, adding emphasis the same way throughout.

3. Click cell **A3**, click the **Italics button** 🅘 on the Formatting toolbar, then click 🅱
The word "Type" appears in boldface italic type. Notice that the Bold, Italics, and Underline buttons are selected.

4. Click 🅘
Excel removes italics from cell A3 but the bold and underline formatting attributes remain.

QuickTip
Use formatting shortcuts on any selected range: [Ctrl][B] to bold, [Ctrl][I] to italicize, and [Ctrl][U] to underline.

5. Select the range **B3:J3**, then click 🅱
Bold formatting is added to the rest of the labels in the column headings. The title would look better if it were centered over the data columns.

6. Select the range **A1:J1**, then click the **Merge and Center button** on the Formatting toolbar
The Merge and Center button creates one cell out of the 10 cells across the row, then centers the text in that newly created large cell. The title "MediaLoft NYC Advertising Expenses" is centered across the 10 columns you selected. You can change the alignment within individual cells using toolbar buttons; you can split merged cells into their original components by selecting the merged cells, then clicking.

QuickTip
To clear all formatting, click Edit on the menu bar, point to Clear, then click Formats.

7. Select the range **A3:J3**, then click the **Center button** on the Formatting toolbar
Compare your screen to Figure C-7. Although they may be difficult to read, notice that all the headings are centered within their cells.

8. Click the **Save button** on the Standard toolbar

 CLUES TO USE

Rotating and indenting cell entries
In addition to applying fonts and formatting attributes, you can rotate or indent cell data within a cell to further change its appearance. You can rotate text within a cell by altering its alignment. To change alignment, select the cells you want to modify, click Format on the menu bar, click Cells, then click the Alignment tab. Click a position in the Orientation box, or type a number in the degrees text box to change from the default horizontal alignment, then click OK. You can indent cell contents using the Increase Indent button on the Formatting toolbar, which moves cell contents to the right one space, or the Decrease Indent button, which moves cell contents to the left one space.

▶ EXCEL C-6   **FORMATTING A WORKSHEET**

Hints as well as troubleshooting advice, right where you need it – next to the step itself.

Quickly accessible summaries of key terms, toolbar buttons, or keyboard alternatives connected with the lesson material. Students can refer easily to this information when working on their own projects at a later time.

Every lesson features large, full-color representations of what the screen should look like as students complete the numbered steps.

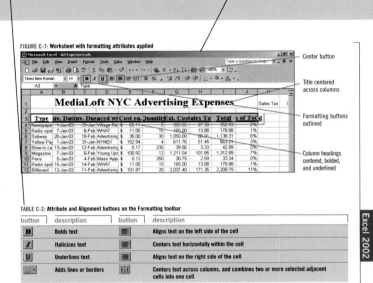

FIGURE C-7: Worksheet with formatting attributes applied

Center button

Title centered across columns

Formatting buttons outlined

Column headings centered, bolded, and underlined

TABLE C-2: Attribute and Alignment buttons on the Formatting toolbar

button	description	button	description
B	Bolds text		Aligns text on the left side of the cell
I	Italicizes text		Centers text horizontally within the cell
U	Underlines text		Aligns text on the right side of the cell
	Adds lines or borders		Centers text across columns, and combines two or more selected adjacent cells into one cell

Excel 2002

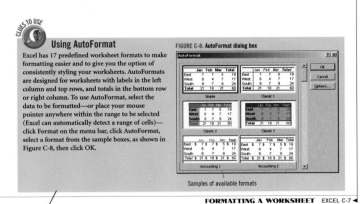

CLUES TO USE

Using AutoFormat

Excel has 17 predefined worksheet formats to make formatting easier and to give you the option of consistently styling your worksheets. AutoFormats are designed for worksheets with labels in the left column and top rows, and totals in the bottom row or right column. To use AutoFormat, select the data to be formatted—or place your mouse pointer anywhere within the range to be selected (Excel can automatically detect a range of cells)—click Format on the menu bar, click AutoFormat, select a format from the sample boxes, as shown in Figure C-8, then click OK.

FIGURE C-8: AutoFormat dialog box

Samples of available formats

FORMATTING A WORKSHEET EXCEL C-7 ◄

Clues to Use boxes provide concise information that either expands on the major lesson skill or describes an independent task that in some way relates to the major lesson skill.

The pages are numbered according to unit. C indicates the unit, 7 indicates the page.

► **Is this book MOUS Certified?**

When used in conjunction with *Microsoft Excel 2002 – Illustrated Intermediate*, this book covers the Core objectives for Excel. When used in conjunction with *Microsoft Excel 2002 – Illustrated Intermediate* and *Advanced*, this book covers the Core and Expert objectives for Excel. When used in this sequence, these titles have received certification approval as courseware for the MOUS program. See the inside front cover for more information on other Illustrated titles meeting MOUS certification.

The first page of each unit includes ⌊MOUS⌉ symbols to indicate which skills covered in the unit are MOUS skills. A grid in the back of the book lists all the exam objectives and cross-references them with the lessons and exercises.

► **What online content solutions are available to accompany this book?**

Visit www.course.com for more information on our online content for Illustrated titles. Options include:

MyCourse.com

Need a quick, simple tool to help you manage your course? Try MyCourse.com, the easiest to use, most flexible syllabus and content management tool available. MyCourse.com offers you brand new content, including Topic Reviews, Extra Case Projects, and Quizzes, to accompany this book.

WebCT

Course Technology and WebCT have partnered to provide you with the highest quality online resources and Web-based tools for your class. Course Technology offers content for this book to help you create your WebCT class, such as a suggested Syllabus, Lecture Notes, Practice Test questions, and more.

Blackboard

Course Technology and Blackboard have also partnered to provide you with the highest quality online resources and Web-based tools for your class. Course Technology offers content for this book to help you create your Blackboard class, such as a suggested Syllabus, Lecture Notes, Practice Test questions, and more.

Instructor Resources

The Instructor's Resource Kit (IRK) CD is Course Technology's way of putting the resources and information needed to teach and learn effectively into your hands. All the components are available on the IRK, (pictured below), and many of the resources can be downloaded from www.course.com.

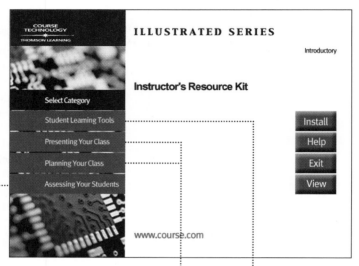

ASSESSING YOUR STUDENTS

Solution Files
Solution Files are Project Files completed with comprehensive sample answers. Use these files to evaluate your students' work. Or, distribute electronically or in hard copy so students can verify their own work.

ExamView
ExamView is a powerful testing software package that allows you to create and administer printed, computer (LAN-based), and Internet exams. ExamView includes hundreds of questions that correspond to the topics covered in this text, enabling students to generate detailed study guides that include page references for further review. The computer-based and Internet testing components allow students to take exams at their computers, and also save you time by grading each exam automatically.

PRESENTING YOUR CLASS

Figure Files
Figure Files contain all the figures from the book in .jpg format. Use the figure files to create transparency masters or in a PowerPoint presentation.

STUDENT TOOLS

Project Files and Project Files List
To complete most of the units in this book, your students will need the **Project Files** from the disk in the back of the book. Instruct students to use the **Project Files List** at the end of the book. This list gives instructions on copying and organizing files.

PLANNING YOUR CLASS

Annotated Instructor's Editions
For each unit, we have provided an electronic pdf document of the unit with annotations located to the left of the page. The annotations include discussion questions, tips, further clarification on difficult topics, and more. You can refer to the pdf file electronically to come up to speed quickly on the skills to cover in class, or print the pdf file for easy reference. An Instructor's Manual (in Word format) is also available, containing solutions, extra Independent Challenges, and other helpful resources.

Course Outlines
Use the Course Outline to plan your day. The Outline includes suggested times for each unit as well as time for breaks and lunch, to complete the Basic, Intermediate, or Advanced skills in one training day. You can customize it to suit your needs and use it as a handout.

SAM, Skills Assessment Manager for Microsoft Office XP
SAM is the most powerful Office XP assessment and reporting tool that will help you gain a true understanding of your students' proficiency in Microsoft Word, Excel, Access, and PowerPoint 2002. (Available separately from the IRK CD.)

TOM, Training Online Manager for Microsoft Office XP
TOM is Course Technology's MOUS-approved training tool for Microsoft Office XP. Available via the World Wide Web and CD-ROM, TOM allows students to actively learn Office XP concepts and skills by delivering realistic practice through both guided and self-directed simulated instruction.

Contents

Illustrated Series Vision
Preface

Read This Before You Begin

Software Information and Required Installation

This book was written and tested using Microsoft Office XP - Professional Edition, with a typical installation on Microsoft Windows 2000, with Internet Explorer 5.0 or higher. There are several instances where, in order to cover a software feature clearly, an additional feature not part of the typical installation is referenced. To insure that all the steps and exercises can be completed as written, make sure the following features are available before beginning this unit: Excel Unit A (page A-8): Using Excel Templates (Clues to Use).

What are Project Files?

To complete many of the units in this book, you need to use Project Files. You use a Project File, which contains a partially completed document used in an exercise, so you don't have to type in all the information you need in the document. Your instructor will either provide you with a copy of the Project Files or ask you to make your own copy. Detailed instructions on how to organize you files, as well as a complete listing of all the files you'll need and will create, can be found in the back of the book (look for the yellow pages) in the Project Files List.

Why is my screen different from the book?

1. Your Desktop components and some dialog box options might be different if you are using an operating system other than Windows 2000

2. Depending on your computer hardware capabilities and the Windows Display settings on your computer, you may notice the following differences:
   - Your screen may look larger or smaller because of your screen resolution (the height and width of your screen)
   - The colors of the title bar in your screen may be a solid blue, and the cells in Excel may appear different from the purple and gray because of your color settings

3. Depending on your Office settings, your toolbars may display on a single row and your menus may display with a shortened list of frequently used commands. Office menus and toolbars can modify themselves to your working style by displaying only the most frequently used buttons and menu commands.

Toolbars in one row

To view buttons not currently displayed, click a Toolbar Options button ⯈ at the end of either the Standard or Formatting toolbar. To view the full list of menu commands, click the double arrow at the bottom of the menu.

In order to have your toolbars display on two rows, showing all buttons, and to have the full menus display, you must turn off the personalized menus and toolbars feature. Click tools on the menu bar, Click Customize, select the show Standard and Formatting toolbars on two rows and Always show full menus check boxes on the Options tab, then click Close. This book assumes you are displaying toolbars on two rows and full menus.

Toolbars on two rows

Unit
A

Getting
Started with Excel 2002

Objectives

► **Define spreadsheet software**
► **Start Excel 2002**
► **View the Excel window**
⌐MOUS⌐ ► **Open and save a workbook**
⌐MOUS⌐ ► **Enter labels and values**
⌐MOUS⌐ ► **Name and move a sheet**
⌐MOUS⌐ ► **Preview and print a worksheet**
► **Get Help**
► **Close a workbook and exit Excel**

In this unit, you will learn how to start Microsoft Excel 2002 and identify elements in the Excel window. You will also learn how to open and save existing files, enter data in a worksheet, manipulate worksheets, and use the extensive Help system. ✒ Jim Fernandez is the office manager at MediaLoft, a nationwide chain of bookstore cafés selling books, CDs, DVDs, and videos. MediaLoft cafés sell coffee and pastries. Jim wants you to help him use Excel to analyze a worksheet summarizing budget information for the MediaLoft Café in the New York City store.

Defining Spreadsheet Software

Microsoft Excel is an electronic spreadsheet program that runs on Windows computers. You use an **electronic spreadsheet** to produce professional-looking documents that perform numeric calculations rapidly and accurately. These calculations are updated automatically so that accurate information is always available. See Table A-1 for common ways spreadsheets are used in business. The electronic spreadsheet that you produce when using Excel is also referred to as a **worksheet**. Individual worksheets are stored within a **workbook**, which is a file with the .xls file extension. Each new workbook contains three worksheets. Jim uses Excel extensively to track MediaLoft finances. Figure A-1 shows a budget worksheet that Jim created using pencil and paper, while Figure A-2 shows the same worksheet Jim created using Excel.

The advantages of using Excel include:

► Enter data quickly and accurately

With Excel, you can enter information faster and more accurately than with pencil and paper. For example, in the MediaLoft NYC Café budget, certain expenses, such as rent, cleaning supplies, and products supplied on a yearly contract (coffee, creamers, sweeteners), remain constant for the year. You can copy the expenses that don't change from quarter to quarter, and then use Excel to calculate Total Expenses and Net Income for each quarter by supplying the data and formulas.

► Recalculate data easily

Fixing typing errors or updating data using Excel is easy, and the results of a changed entry are recalculated automatically. For example, if you receive updated expense figures for Quarter 4, you enter the new numbers and Excel recalculates the worksheet.

► Perform a what-if analysis

The Excel ability to change data and let you quickly view the recalculated results makes it a powerful decision-making tool. For instance, if the salary budget per quarter is increased to $14,500, you can enter the new figure into the worksheet and immediately see the impact on the overall budget. Any time you use a worksheet to ask the question "what if?" you are performing a **what-if analysis**.

► Change the appearance of information

Excel provides powerful features for making information visually appealing and easy to understand. For example, you can use boldface type and colored or shaded text headings or numbers to emphasize important worksheet data and trends.

► Create charts

Excel makes it easy to create charts based on worksheet information. Charts are updated automatically as data changes. The worksheet in Figure A-2 includes a 3-D pie chart that shows the distribution of the budget expenses for the MediaLoft NYC Café.

► Share information with other users

Because everyone at MediaLoft is now using Microsoft Office, it's easy for them to share worksheet data. For example, you can complete the MediaLoft budget that your manager started creating in Excel. Simply access the files you need or want to share through the network or from a disk, or through the use of online collaboration tools (such as intranets and the Internet), and then make any changes or additions.

► Create new worksheets from existing ones quickly

It's easy to take an existing Excel worksheet and quickly modify it to create a new one. When you are ready to create next year's budget, you can open the file for this year's budget, save it with a new filename, and use the existing data as a starting point. An Excel file can also be created using a special format called a **template**, which lets you open a new file based on an existing workbook's design and/or content. Office comes with many prepared templates you can use.

FIGURE A-1: Traditional paper worksheet

	Qtr 1	Qtr 2	Qtr 3	Qtr 4	Total
MediaLoft NYC Café Budget					
Net Sales	56,000	84,000	72,000	79,000	291,000
Expenses					
Salary	14,500	14,500	14,500	14,500	58,000
Rent	4,000	4,000	4,000	4,000	16,000
Advertising	3,750	8,000	3,750	3,750	19,250
Cleansers	1,500	1,500	1,500	1,500	6,000
Pastries	2,500	2,500	2,500	2,500	10,000
Milk/Cream	1,000	1,000	1,000	1,000	4,000
Coffee/Tea	4,700	4,750	4,750	4,750	18,950
Sweeteners	300	300	300	300	1,200
Total Expenses	32,250	36,550	32,300	32,300	133,400
Net Income	23,750	47,450	39,700	46,700	157,600

FIGURE A-2: Excel worksheet

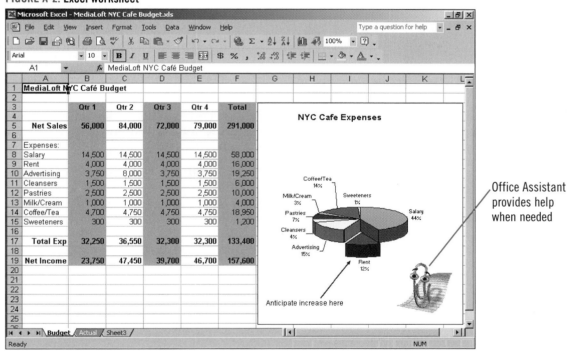

Office Assistant provides help when needed

TABLE A-1: Common business uses for electronic spreadsheets

spreadsheets are used to	by
Maintain values	Calculating numbers
Represent values graphically	Creating charts based on worksheet figures
Create consecutively numbered pages using multiple workbook sheets	Printing reports containing workbook sheets
Organize data	Sorting data in ascending or descending order
Analyze data	Creating data summaries and short-lists using PivotTables or AutoFilters
Create what-if data scenarios	Using variable values to investigate and sample different outcomes

Excel 2002

Starting Excel 2002

To start any Windows program, you use the Start button on the taskbar. A slightly different procedure might be required for computers on a network and those that use Windows-enhancing utilities. If you need assistance, ask your instructor or technical support person. ✐ Jim is ready to begin work on the budget for the MediaLoft Café in New York City. He begins by starting Excel.

Steps

1. Point to the **Start button** 🏁Start on the taskbar

The Start button is on the left side of the taskbar. You use it to start programs on your computer.

2. Click 🏁Start

Microsoft Excel is located in the Programs folder, which is at the top of the Start menu, as shown in Figure A-3.

3. Point to **Programs**

The Programs menu opens. All the programs on your computer, including Microsoft Excel, are listed on this menu. See Figure A-4. Your program menu might look different, depending on the programs installed on your computer.

Trouble?

If you don't see the Microsoft Excel icon, see your instructor or technical support person.

4. Click the **Microsoft Excel program icon** on the Programs menu

Excel opens and a blank worksheet appears. In the next lesson, you will learn about the elements of the Excel worksheet window.

5. If necessary, click the **Maximize button** 🔲 on the title bar

FIGURE A-3: **Start menu**

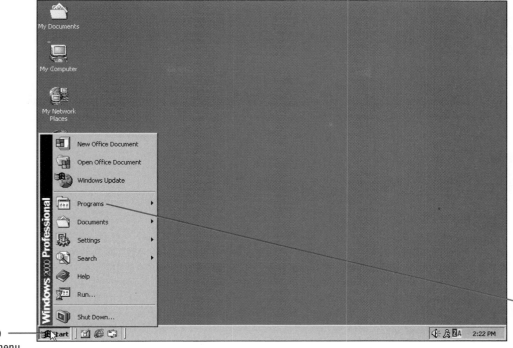

Click here to open Start menu

Microsoft Excel located in this folder

FIGURE A-4: **Programs list**

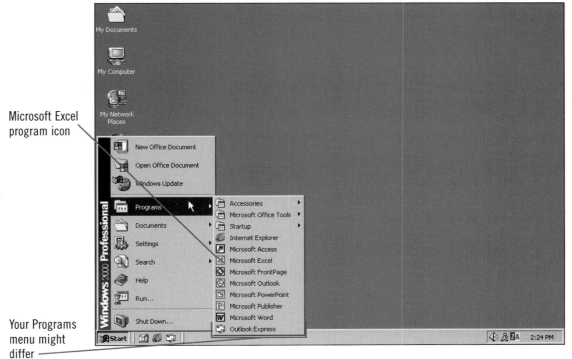

Microsoft Excel program icon

Your Programs menu might differ

Excel 2002

Viewing the Excel Window

When you start Excel, the **worksheet window** appears on your screen. The worksheet window includes the tools that enable you to create and work with worksheets. ▰▰▰ Jim needs to familiarize himself with the Excel worksheet window and its elements before he starts working with the budget worksheet. Compare the descriptions below to the elements shown in Figure A-5.

Details

► The **worksheet window** contains a grid of columns and rows. Columns are labeled alphabetically (A, B, C, etc.) and rows are labeled numerically (1, 2, 3, etc.). The worksheet window displays only a small fraction of the whole worksheet, which has a total of 256 columns and 65,536 rows. The intersection of a column and a row is called a **cell**. Cells can contain text, numbers, formulas, or a combination of all three. Every cell has its own unique location or **cell address**, which is identified by the coordinates of the intersecting column and row. For example, the cell address of the cell in the upper-left corner of a worksheet is A1. The **new workbook pane** appears to the right of the worksheet window and lets you quickly open new or existing workbooks. The **Task pane list arrow** lets you display other panes.

Trouble?

If your screen does not display cells in purple and gray as shown in the figure, ask your technical support person to check your Windows color settings.

► The **cell pointer** is a dark rectangle that outlines the cell you are working in. This cell is called the **active cell**. In Figure A-5, the cell pointer is located at A1, so A1 is the active cell. The column and row headings for the active cell are purple; inactive column and row headings are gray. To activate a different cell, just click any other cell or press the arrow keys on your keyboard to move the cell pointer elsewhere.

► The **title bar** displays the program name (Microsoft Excel) and the filename of the open worksheet (in this case the default filename, Book1). As shown in Figure A-5, the title bar also contains a control menu box, a Close button, and resizing buttons, which are common to all Windows programs.

► The **menu bar** contains menus from which you choose Excel commands. As with all Windows programs, you can choose a menu command by clicking it with the mouse pointer or by pressing [Alt] plus the underlined letter in the menu command name. When you click a menu, only a short list of commonly used commands may appear at first; you can wait or click the double arrows at the bottom of the menu to see expanded menus with more commands.

► The **name box** displays the active cell address. In Figure A-5, "A1" appears in the name box, indicating that A1 is the active cell.

► The **formula bar** allows you to enter or edit data in the worksheet.

► The **toolbars** contain buttons for frequently used Excel commands. The **Standard toolbar** is located just below the menu bar and contains buttons that perform actions within the worksheet. The **Formatting toolbar**—beneath the Standard toolbar—contains buttons that change the worksheet's appearance. Each button contains an image representing its function. For instance, the Print button contains an image of a printer. To choose any button, click it with the left mouse button.

► **Sheet tabs** below the worksheet grid let you keep your work in a collection called a **workbook**. Each workbook contains three worksheets by default and can contain a maximum of 255 sheets. Sheet tabs allow you to name your worksheets with meaningful names. **Sheet tab scrolling buttons** help you display hidden worksheets.

► The **status bar** is located at the bottom of the Excel window. The left side of the status bar provides a brief description of the active command or task in progress. The right side of the status bar shows the status of important keys such as [Caps Lock] and [Num Lock].

FIGURE A-5: Excel worksheet window elements

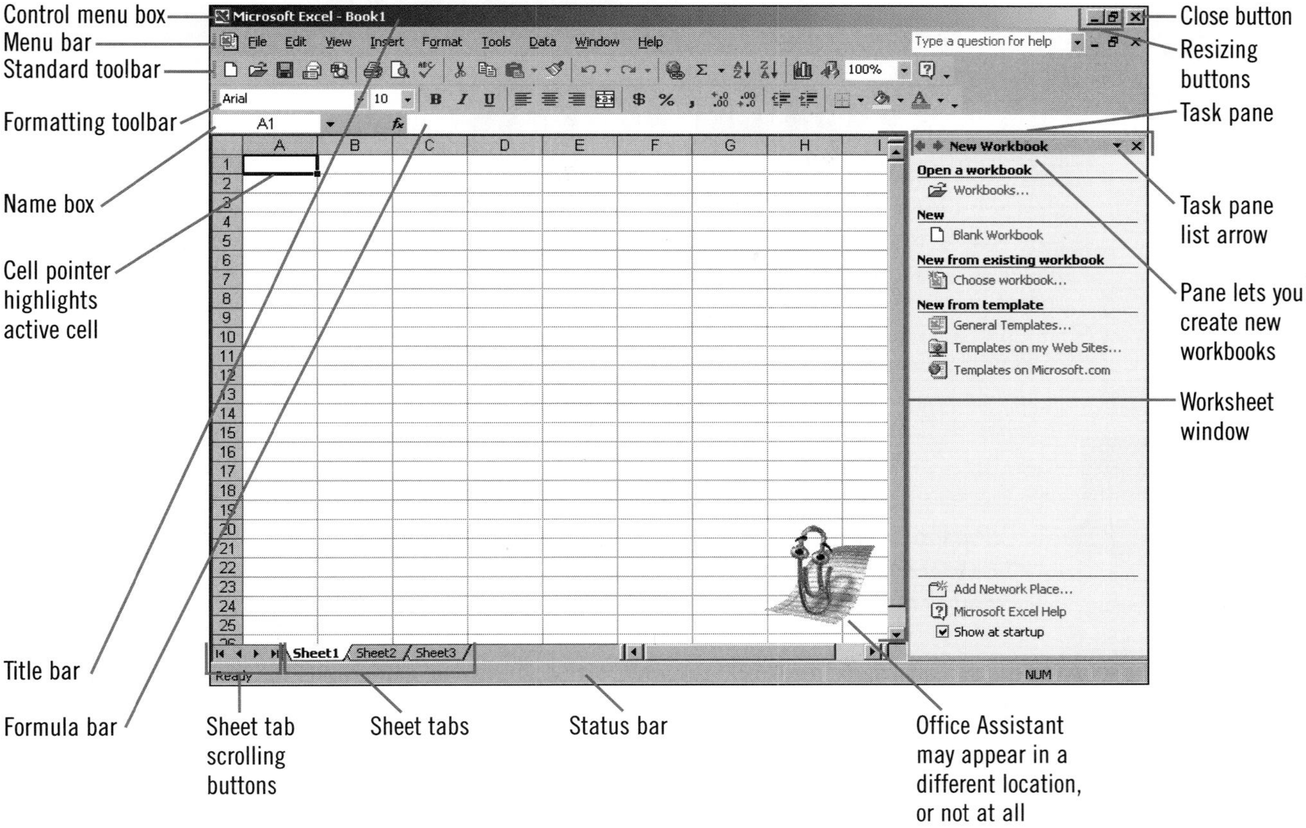

Control menu box

Menu bar

Standard toolbar

Formatting toolbar

Name box

Cell pointer
highlights
active cell

Title bar

Formula bar

Sheet tab
scrolling
buttons

Sheet tabs

Status bar

Close button

Resizing
buttons

Task pane

Task pane
list arrow

Pane lets you
create new
workbooks

Worksheet
window

Office Assistant
may appear in a
different location,
or not at all

Working with toolbars and menus in Excel 2002

Although you can configure Excel so that your toolbars and menus modify themselves to conform to your working style, the lessons in this book assume you have turned off personalized menus and toolbars and are working with all menu commands and toolbar buttons displayed. When you use personalized toolbars, the Standard and Formatting toolbars appear on the same row and display only the most frequently used buttons, as shown in Figure A-6. To use a button that is not visible on a toolbar, you click the Toolbar Options button at the end of the toolbar, then click the button on the Toolbar Options list. As you work, Excel adds the buttons you use to the visible toolbars and drops the buttons you don't often use to the Toolbar Options list. Similarly, Excel menus adjust to your work habits, so that the commands you use most often appear on shortened menus. You can see all the menu commands by clicking the double arrows at the bottom of a menu. It is often easier to work with full toolbars and menus displayed. To turn off personalized toolbars and menus, click Tools on the menu bar, click Customize, on the Options tab select the Show Standard and Formatting toolbars on two rows and Always show full menus check boxes, and then click Close. The Standard and Formatting toolbars appear on separate rows and display all the buttons, and the menus display the complete list of menu commands. (You can quickly display the toolbars on two rows by clicking a Toolbar Options button and then clicking Show Buttons on Two Rows.)

FIGURE A-6: Toolbars in one row

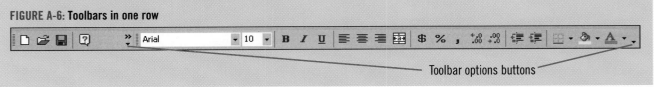

Toolbar options buttons

Excel 2002

Excel 2002

Opening and Saving a Workbook

Sometimes it's more efficient to create a new worksheet by modifying one that already exists. This saves you from having to retype information from previous work. Throughout this book, you will create new workbooks by opening a file from the location where your Project Files are stored, using the Save As command to create a copy of the file with a new name, and then modifying the new file by following the lesson steps. Use the Save command to store changes made to an existing file. It is a good idea to save your work every 10 or 15 minutes and before printing. Saving the files with new names keeps your original Project Files intact, in case you have to start the unit over again or you wish to repeat an exercise. ✐ Jim wants you to complete the New York City MediaLoft Café budget that a member of the accounting staff has been working on.

Steps

QuickTip

You can also click the Open button 📂 on the Standard toolbar.

1. Click More Workbooks in the New Workbook task pane

The Open dialog box opens. See Figure A-7. If no workbooks have been opened on your computer, the command will read "Workbooks."

QuickTip

If you don't see the three-letter extension .xls on the filenames in the Open dialog box, don't worry. Windows can be set up to display or not to display the file extensions.

2. Click the Look in list arrow, then click the drive and folder where your Project Files are located

The Look in list arrow lets you navigate to folders and disk drives on your computer. A list of your Project Files appears in the Open dialog box.

3. Click the file EX A-1, then click Open

The workbook file EX A-1 opens. The new workbook pane no longer appears.

QuickTip

You can create a new folder from within the Save As dialog box by clicking 📁 on the dialog box toolbar, typing a name in the Name text box, then clicking OK. To open a file from a folder you create, double-click folders or use the Look in list arrow in the Open dialog box to open the folder, click the filename, then click Open.

4. Click File on the menu bar, then click Save As

The Save As dialog box opens, displaying the drive where your Project Files are stored.

5. In the File name text box, select the current filename (if necessary), type MediaLoft Cafe Budget, as shown in Figure A-8, then click Save

Both the Save As dialog box and the file EX A-1 close, and a duplicate file named MediaLoft Cafe Budget opens, as shown in Figure A-9. The Office Assistant may or may not appear on your screen.

Creating a new workbook

You can create your own worksheets from scratch by opening a new workbook. To create a new workbook, click the New button 📄 on the Standard toolbar. You can also use the New Workbook pane (located on the right side of the screen) to open a new file. Click the Blank Workbook button 📄 in the New Workbook pane, and a new workbook will open. Each new workbook automatically contains 3 sheets, although you can insert as many as you need.

FIGURE A-7: Open dialog box

Your folder contents might differ

Your files and folders appear here

Selected filename will appear here

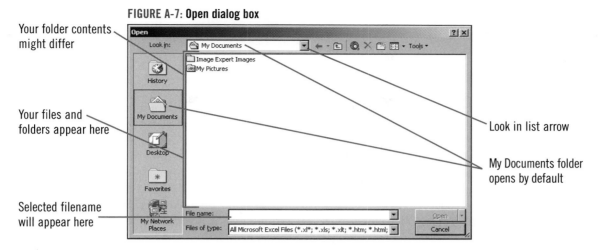

Look in list arrow

My Documents folder opens by default

FIGURE A-8: Save As dialog box

Your list of files might differ

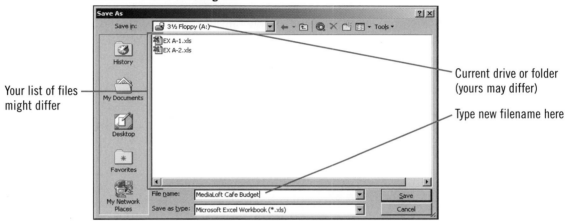

Current drive or folder (yours may differ)

Type new filename here

FIGURE A-9: MediaLoft Café Budget workbook

Purple column and row headers define active cell

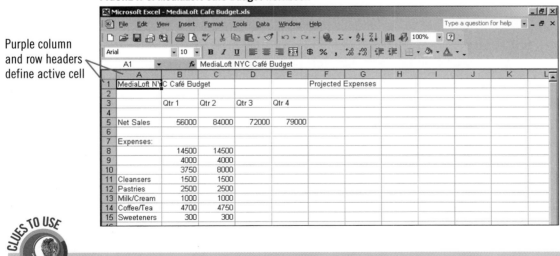

Opening a workbook using a template

You can create a workbook by entering data and formats into a blank workbook, or you can use predesigned workbooks called templates that are included with Excel. Templates let you automatically create workbooks such as balance sheets, expense statements, loan amortizations, sales invoices, or timecards. Templates save you time because they contain labels, values, formulas, and formatting. To open a new document based on a template, click General Templates from the New Workbook task pane, save it under a new name, then add your own information. You may need to have the Office CD available to install the templates.

Excel 2002

Entering Labels and Values

Labels help you identify the data in worksheet rows and columns, making your worksheet more readable and understandable. Try to enter all labels in your worksheet before entering the data. Labels can contain text and numerical information not used in calculations, such as dates, times, or addresses. Labels are left-aligned by default. **Values**, which include numbers, formulas, and functions, are used in calculations. Excel recognizes an entry as a value when it is a number or begins with special symbols: +, -, =, @, #, or $. Because Excel treats labels and values differently, you can have a label such as '2003 Sales' without affecting values used in a totals column. All values are right-aligned by default. When a cell contains both text and numbers it is not a valid formula; Excel recognizes the entry as a label. Jim wants you to enter labels identifying the rest of the expense categories, and the values for Qtr 3 and Qtr 4 into the MediaLoft Café Budget worksheet.

Steps 1 2 3 4

1. **Click cell A8 to make it the active cell**
   Notice that the cell address A8 appears in the name box. As you work, the mouse pointer takes on a variety of appearances, depending on where it is and what Excel is doing. Table A-2 lists and identifies some mouse pointers. The labels in cells A8:A15 identify the expenses.

2. **Type Salary, as shown in Figure A-10, then click the Enter button ☑ on the formula bar**
   As you type, the word "Enter" appears in the status bar. Clicking the Enter button indicates that you are finished typing or changing your entry, and the word "Ready" appears in the status bar. Because the cell is still selected, its contents still appear in the formula bar. You can also confirm a cell entry by pressing [Enter], [Tab], or one of the keyboard arrow keys. These three methods also select an adjacent cell. To confirm an entry and leave the same cell selected, you can press [Ctrl][Enter]. If a label does not fit in a cell, Excel displays the remaining characters in the next cell to the right, as long as it is empty. Otherwise, the label is **truncated**, or cut off.

3. **Click cell A9, type Rent, press [Enter] to confirm the entry and move the cell pointer to cell A10, type Advertising in cell A10, then press [Enter]**
   The remaining expense values have to be added to the worksheet.

4. **Click cell D8, press and hold down the left mouse button, drag ✛ to cell E8 then down to cell E15, then release the mouse button**
   You have selected a **range**, which is two or more adjacent cells. The active cell is still cell D8, and the cells in the range are shaded in purple.

5. **Type 14500, press [Enter], type 4000 in cell D9, press [Enter], type 3750 in cell D10, press [Enter], type 1500 in cell D11, press [Enter], type 2500 in cell D12, press [Enter], type 1000 in cell D13, press [Enter], type 4750 in cell D14, press [Enter], type 300 in cell D15, then press [Enter]**
   You will often enter data in multiple columns and rows; selecting a range makes working with data entry easier because pressing [Enter] makes the next cell in the range active. You have entered all the values in the Qtr 3 column, as shown in Figure A-11. The cell pointer is now in cell E8.

6. **Using Figure A-11 as a guide, type the remaining values for cells E8 through E15**
   Before confirming a cell entry, you can click the Cancel button on the formula bar or press [Esc] to cancel or delete the entry. Notice that the AutoCalculate area in the status bar displays "Sum=64550," which is the sum of the figures in the selected range. This sum changes if you change any of the numbers in the selected range.

7. **Click cell D8, type 14550, press [Enter], then select cells D8:E15**
   Notice that the AutoCalculate area in the status bar now says "Sum=64600".

8. **Press [Ctrl][Home] to return to cell A1**

9. **Click the Save button 🖫 on the Standard toolbar**
   You can also press [Ctrl][S] to save a worksheet.

Trouble?

If you notice a mistake in a cell entry after entering it, double-click the cell, use [Backspace] or [Delete], make your corrections, then press [Enter]. You can also click Edit on the menu bar, point to Clear, then click Contents to remove a cell's contents.

QuickTip

To enter a number that will not be used as part of a calculation, such as a telephone number, type an apostrophe (') before the number.

FIGURE A-10: Worksheet with first label entered

Enter button

Name box

Cancel button

Formula bar

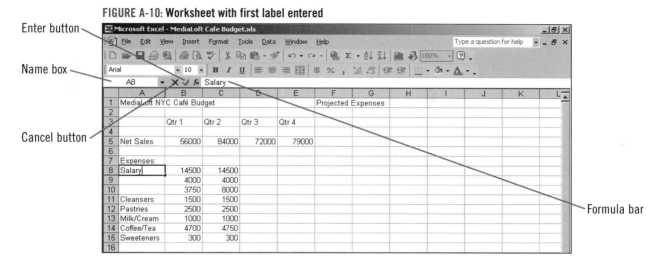

FIGURE A-11: Worksheet with new labels and values

Type these values

Labels entered

Values entered

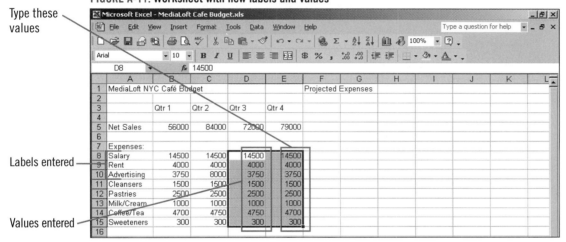

TABLE A-2: Commonly used pointers

name	pointer	use to
Normal		Select a cell or range; indicates Ready mode
Copy		Create a duplicate of the selected cell(s)
Fill handle		Create an alphanumeric series in a range
I-beam		Edit contents of formula bar
Move		Change the location of the selected cell(s)

CLUES TO USE

Navigating a worksheet

With over a million cells available to you, it is important to know how to move around, or **navigate**, a worksheet. You can use the arrow keys on the keyboard ([↑] [↓] [←] or [→]) to move a cell or two at a time, or use [Page Up] or [Page Down] to move a screenful at a time. To move a screen to the left press [Alt][Page Up]; to move a screen to the right press

[Alt][Page Down]. You can also use the mouse pointer to click the desired cell. If the desired cell is not visible in the worksheet window, use the scroll bars or the Go To command on the Edit menu to move the location into view. To return to the first active cell in a worksheet, click cell A1, or press [Ctrl][Home].

Excel 2002

Naming and Moving a Sheet

Each workbook initially contains three worksheets, named Sheet1, Sheet2, and Sheet3. When you open a workbook, the first worksheet is the active sheet. To move from sheet to sheet, you can click any sheet tab at the bottom of the worksheet window. The sheet tab scrolling buttons, located to the left of the sheet tabs, allow you to display hidden sheet tabs. To make it easier to identify the sheets in a workbook, you can rename each sheet, add color to the tabs, and then organize them in a logical way. The sheet name appears on the sheet tab. For instance, to better track performance goals, you could name each workbook sheet for an individual salesperson; then you could move the sheets so they appeared in alphabetical order. ✐ Jim wants to be able to easily identify the actual expenses and the projected expenses. He wants you to name two sheets in his workbook, add color to distinguish them, then change their order.

Steps

1. **Click the Sheet2 tab**
   Sheet2 becomes active; this is the worksheet that contains the actual quarterly expenses. Its tab moves to the front, and Sheet1 moves to the background.

2. **Click the Sheet1 tab**
   Sheet1, which contains the projected expenses, becomes active again. Once you have confirmed which sheet is which, you can assign them each a name that you can easily remember.

> **QuickTip**
> You can also rename a sheet by right-clicking the tab, clicking Rename, typing the new name, then pressing [Enter].

3. **Double-click the Sheet2 tab**
   Sheet 2 becomes the active sheet with the default sheet name ("Sheet2") selected.

4. **Type Actual, then press [Enter]**
   The new name automatically replaces the default name in the tab. Worksheet names can have up to 31 characters, including spaces and punctuation.

5. **Right-click the Actual tab, then click Tab Color**
   The Format Tab Color dialog box appears, as shown in Figure A-12.

> **QuickTip**
> To delete a worksheet, select the worksheet you want to delete, click Edit on the menu bar, then click Delete sheet. To insert a worksheet, click Insert on the menu bar, then click Worksheet.

6. **Click the color red (first column, third row), click OK, double-click the Sheet1 tab, type Projected, then press [Enter]**
   Notice that when you renamed Sheet1, the color of the entire Actual tab changed to red. Jim decides to rearrange the order of the sheets, so that Actual comes before Projected.

7. **Click the Actual sheet tab and hold down the mouse button, then drag it to the left of the Projected sheet tab**
   As you drag, the pointer changes to ▯, the sheet relocation pointer, and a small, black triangle shows its position. See Figure A-13. The first sheet in the workbook is now the Actual sheet. When you have more worksheets than can appear at once, click the leftmost tab scrolling button to display the first sheet tab; click the rightmost navigation button to display the last sheet tab. The left and right buttons move one sheet in their respective directions.

8. **Click the Projected sheet tab, enter your name in cell A20, then press [Ctrl][Home]**
   Your name identifies your worksheet as yours, which is helpful if you are sharing a printer.

9. **Click the Save button 🖫 on the Standard toolbar**

FIGURE A-12: **Format Tab Color dialog box**

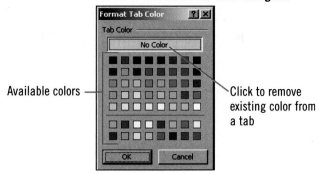

Available colors

Click to remove existing color from a tab

FIGURE A-13: **Moving Actual sheet before Projected sheet**

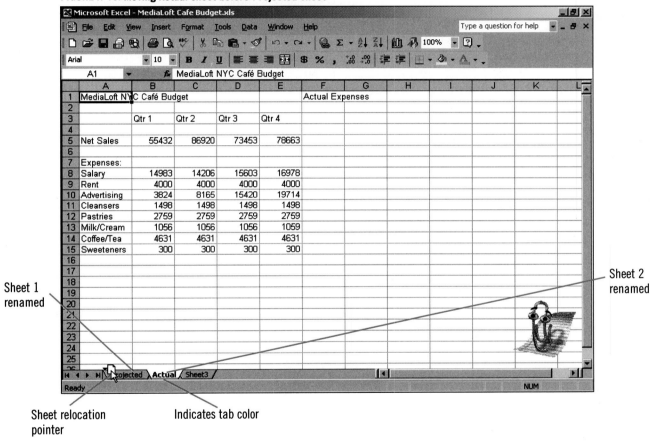

Sheet 1 renamed

Sheet 2 renamed

Sheet relocation pointer

Indicates tab color

Copying worksheets

There are times when you may want to copy a worksheet. To copy it, press [Ctrl] as you drag the sheet tab and release the mouse button before you release [Ctrl]. You can also move and copy worksheets between workbooks. You must have the workbook that you are copying to, as well as the workbook that you are copying from, open. Select the sheet to copy or move, click Edit on the menu bar, then click Move or Copy sheet. Complete the information in the Move or Copy dialog box. Be sure to click the Create a Copy check box if you are copying rather than moving the worksheet. Carefully check your calculation results whenever you move or copy a worksheet.

Excel 2002

Previewing and Printing a Worksheet

After you complete a worksheet, you may want to print it to have a paper copy for reference or to give to others. You can also print a worksheet that is not complete to review your work when you are not at a computer. Before you print a worksheet, you should save any changes. That way, if anything happens to the file as it is being sent to the printer, you will have your latest work saved. Then you should preview it to make sure it will fit on a page the way you want. When you **preview** a worksheet, you see a copy of the worksheet exactly as it will appear on paper. See Table A-3 for a summary of printing tips. ✎ Jim is finished entering the labels and values into the MediaLoft Café budget. He has already saved his changes, so he asks you to preview and print a copy of the worksheet he can review on the way home.

1. **Make sure the printer is on and contains paper**
   If a file is sent to print and the printer is off, an error message appears.

2. **Click the Print Preview button 🔍 on the Standard toolbar**
   A miniature version of the worksheet appears on the screen, as shown in Figure A-14. If your worksheet requires more than one page, you could click the Next button or the Previous button to move between pages. Because your worksheet is only one page, the Next and Previous buttons are dimmed.

> **QuickTip**
>
> To print the worksheet using existing settings without previewing it, click 🖨 on the Standard toolbar.

3. **Click Print**
   The Print dialog box opens, as shown in Figure A-15.

4. **Make sure that the Active Sheet(s) option button is selected in the Print what section and that 1 appears in the Number of copies text box in the Copies section**
   Adjusting the value in the Number of copies text box enables you to print multiple copies. You could also print a selected range by clicking the Selection option button.

> **QuickTip**
>
> After previewing or printing a worksheet, dotted lines appear on the screen indicating individual page breaks in the printout. Page break positions vary with each printer.

5. **Click OK**
   A Printing dialog box appears briefly while the file is sent to the printer. Note that the dialog box contains a Cancel button. You can use it to cancel the print job provided you can catch it before the file is sent to the printer.

TABLE A-3: Worksheet printing tips

before you print	recommendation
Save your work	Make sure your work is saved
Check the printer	Make sure that the printer is turned on and is online, that it has paper, and that there are no error messages or warning signals
Preview the worksheet	Check the formatted image for page breaks, page setup (vertical or horizontal), and overall appearance of the worksheet
Check the printer selection	Look in the Print dialog box to verify that the correct printer is selected
Check the Print what options	Verify that you are printing either the active sheet, the entire workbook, or just a selected range

FIGURE A-14: Print Preview screen

Move to another page

Enlarge the screen image

Print the worksheet

Change print options

Return to worksheet

Zoom pointer

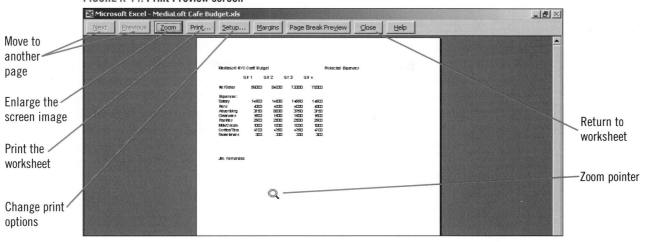

FIGURE A-15: Print dialog box

Your printer may differ

Prints the current worksheet

Indicates the number of copies to be printed

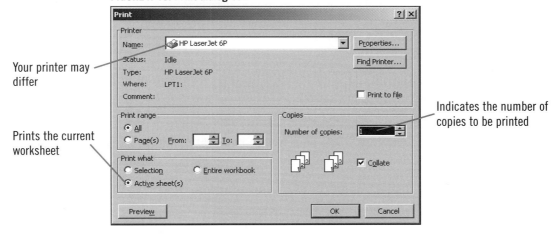

Using Zoom in Print Preview

When you are in the Print Preview window, you can enlarge the image by clicking the Zoom button. You can also position the Zoom pointer ![zoom] over a specific part of the worksheet page, then click it to view that section of the page. Figure A-16 shows a magnified section of a document. While the image is zoomed in, use the scroll bars to view different sections of the page.

FIGURE A-16: Enlarging the preview using Zoom

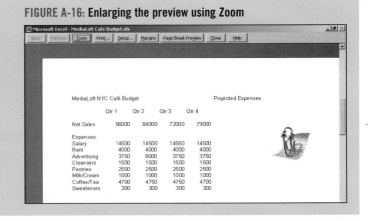

Excel 2002

Getting Help

Excel features an extensive **Help system** that gives you immediate access to definitions, steps, explanations, and useful tips. The animated Office Assistant provides help in two ways. You can type a **keyword**, a representative word on which Excel can search your area of interest, or you can access a question and answer format to research your Help topic. The Office Assistant provides **Office Assistant Tips** (indicated by a light bulb) on the current action you are performing. You can click the light bulb to display a dialog box containing relevant choices that you can refer to as you work. In addition, you can press [F1] at any time to get immediate help. Alternately, the **Ask a Question list arrow** on the menu bar is always available for asking questions. You can click the text box and type a question at any time to display related help topics. Questions from your current Excel session are stored, and you can access them at any time by clicking the Ask a Question list arrow, then clicking the question of interest. ✏️ Jim wants to find out more about ranges so he can work more efficiently with them. He asks you to find more information by using the animated Office Assistant.

QuickTip
If the Office Assistant is displayed, click it to access Help. If it is not displayed, clicking 🔲 opens the Office Assistant. A previous user may have turned off the Office Assistant. To turn it on, click Help on the menu bar, click Show the Office Assistant, then click the Office Assistant to open the dialog balloon.

1. Click the **Microsoft Excel Help button** 🔲 on the Standard toolbar

An Office Assistant dialog balloon opens, asking what you want to do. You can get information by typing a keyword or question in the white box, known as the **query box**. If the text within the query box is highlighted, your text will automatically replace it. The Office Assistant provides help based on the text in the query box.

2. Type **Define a range**

See Figure A-18.

3. Click **Search**

The Office Assistant searches for relevant topics from the Help files in Excel and then displays a list of topics for you to choose from.

QuickTip
Clicking the Print button 🖨 in the Help window prints the information.

4. Click **See More**, then click **Name cells on more than one worksheet**

A Help window containing information about ranges opens, as shown in Figure A-19.

5. Read the text, then click the **Close button** ✖ on the Help window title bar

The Help window closes.

6. Click the Microsoft Excel button on the taskbar to display it, if necessary.

The Office Assistant is no longer visible on the worksheet. Hiding the Office Assistant does not turn it off; it only hides it temporarily.

Changing the Office Assistant

The default Office Assistant character is Clippit, but there are others from which you can choose. To change the appearance of the Office Assistant, right-click the Office Assistant, then click Options. Click the Gallery tab shown in Figure A-17, click the Back and Next buttons until you find an Assistant you want to use, then click OK. (You may need to insert your Microsoft Office CD to perform this task.) Each Office Assistant character makes its own unique sounds. Animate any assistant by right-clicking it, then clicking Animate!

FIGURE A-17: Office Assistant dialog box

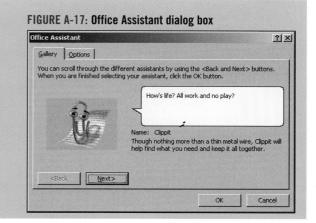

FIGURE A-18: Office Assistant

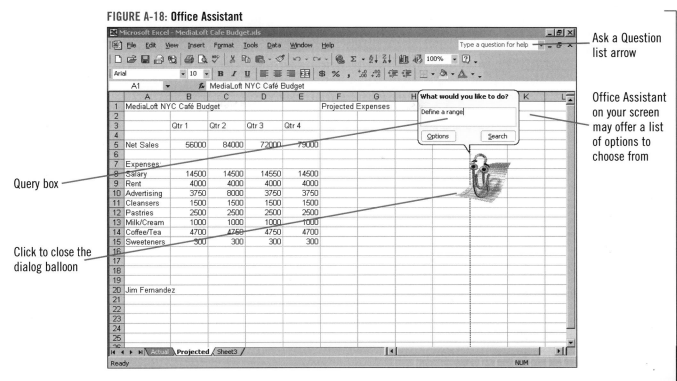

Ask a Question list arrow

Office Assistant on your screen may offer a list of options to choose from

Query box

Click to close the dialog balloon

FIGURE A-19: Help window

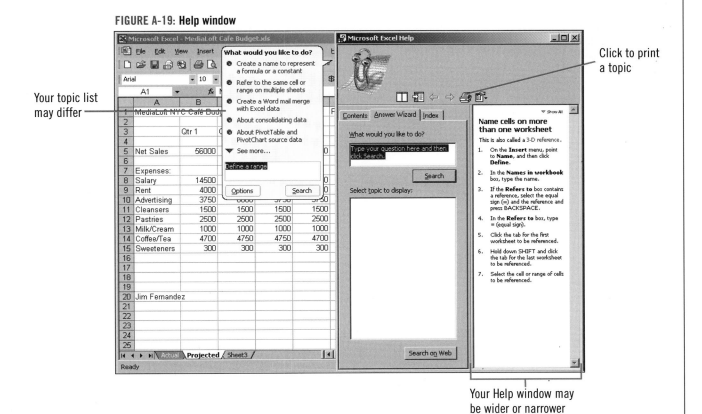

Click to print a topic

Your topic list may differ

Your Help window may be wider or narrower

Excel 2002

Closing a Workbook and Exiting Excel

When you have finished working, you need to save the workbook file and close it. When you have completed all your work in Excel you need to exit the program. You can exit Excel by clicking Exit on the File menu. Jim has completed his work on the MediaLoft Café budget. He wants you to close the workbook and then exit Excel.

Steps 1 2 3 4

1. **Click File on the menu bar**

   The File menu opens. See Figure A-20.

2. **Click Close**

   Excel closes the workbook, asking if you want to save your changes; if you have made any changes be sure to save them. You could also click the workbook Close button instead of using the File menu.

QuickTip

To exit Excel and close several files at once, click Exit on the File menu. Excel will prompt you to save changes to each open workbook before exiting.

3. **Click File on the menu bar, then click Exit**

   You could also click the program Close button to exit the program. Excel closes and you return to the desktop.

FIGURE A-20: Closing a workbook using the File menu

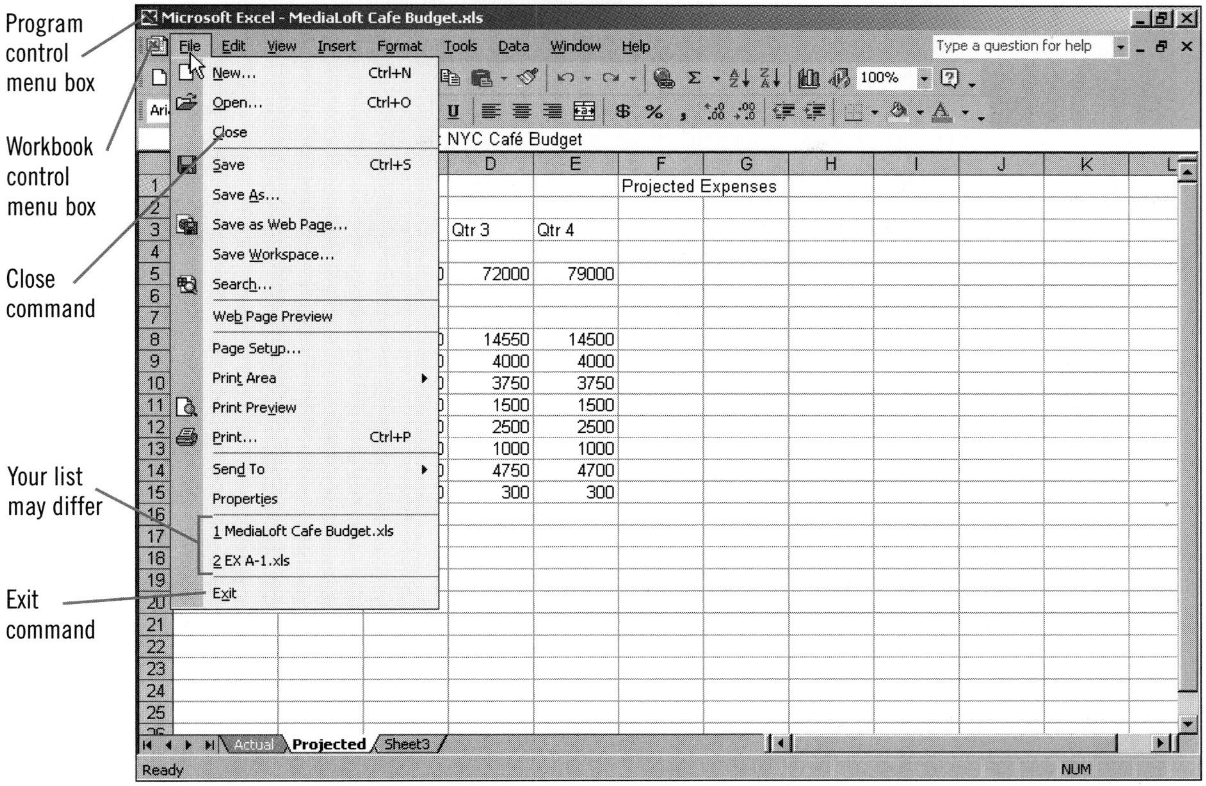

Program control menu box

Workbook control menu box

Close command

Your list may differ

Exit command

Excel 2002

Practice

► Concepts Review

Label the elements of the Excel worksheet window shown in Figure A-21.

FIGURE A-21

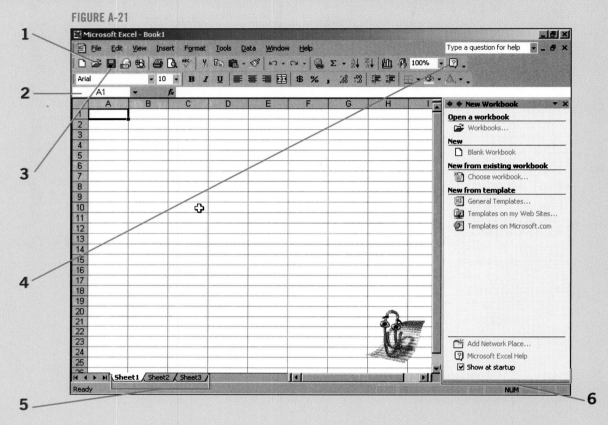

Match each term with the statement that describes it.

7. Cell pointer
8. Formula bar
9. Worksheet window
10. Name box
11. Cell
12. Workbook

a. Area that contains a grid of columns and rows
b. The intersection of a column and row
c. Allows you to enter or edit worksheet data
d. Collection of worksheets
e. Rectangle indicating the active cell
f. Displays the active cell address

Select the best answer from the list of choices.

13. An electronic spreadsheet can perform all of the following tasks, except:
    a. Display information visually.
    b. Calculate data accurately.
    c. Plan worksheet objectives.
    d. Recalculate updated information.

14. Each of the following is true about labels, except:
    a. They are left-aligned by default.
    b. They are not used in calculations.
    c. They are right-aligned by default.
    d. They can include numerical information.

15. **Each of the following is true about values, except:**
    a. They can include labels.
    b. They are right-aligned by default.
    c. They are used in calculations.
    d. They can include formulas.

16. **What symbol is typed before a number to make the number a label?**
    a. "
    b. !
    c. '
    d. ;

17. **You can get Excel Help in any of the following ways, except:**
    a. Clicking Help on the menu bar, then clicking Microsoft Excel Help.
    b. Pressing [F1].
    c. Clicking 🔲.
    d. Minimizing the program window.

18. **The following key(s) can be used to confirm cell entries, except:**
    a. [Enter].
    b. [Tab].
    c. [Esc].
    d. [Ctrl][Enter].

19. **Which button is used to preview a worksheet?**
    a. 🔲
    b. 🔲
    c. 🔲
    d. 🔲

20. **Which feature is used to enlarge a Print Preview view?**
    a. Magnify
    b. Enlarge
    c. Amplify
    d. Zoom

21. **Each of the following is true about the Office Assistant, except:**
    a. It provides tips based on your work habits.
    b. It provides help using a question-and-answer format.
    c. You can change the appearance of the Office Assistant.
    d. It can complete certain tasks for you.

▶ Skills Review

1. **Start Excel 2002.**
    a. Point to **Programs** in the Start menu.
    b. Click the **Microsoft Excel** program icon.
    c. In what area of the Start menu are all the programs on your computer located?
    d. What appears when Excel opens?

2. **Open and save a workbook.**
    a. Open the workbook EX A-2 from the drive and folder where your Project Files are located.
    b. Save the workbook as **MediaLoft Toronto Cafe** using the Save As command on the File menu; use the New Folder button to save it in a new folder called **Toronto** in the drive and folder where your Project Files are located.
    c. Close the file.
    d. Open it again from the new folder you created.
    e. Open a workbook based on the Balance Sheet template: Display the task pane, select General Templates, display the Spreadsheet Solutions tab, then double-click Balance Sheet.
    f. Save the workbook as **MediaLoft Balance Sheet** in the drive and folder where your Project Files are stored, then close the workbook.

TABLE-4: MediaLoft Toronto Café

	On-Hand	Cost Each	Sale Price
Water	32	9.57	
Coffee	52	13.71	
Bread	36	15.22	
Muffins	25	16.99	
Sweets	43	11.72	
Sodas	52	9.61	

3. **Enter labels and values.**
   a. Enter the necessary labels shown in Table A-4.
   b. Enter the values shown in Table A-4.
   c. Clear the contents of cell A9 using the Edit menu, then type **Tea** in cell A9.
   d. Save the workbook using the Save button.

4. **Name and move a sheet.**
   a. Name the Sheet1 tab **Inventory**, then name the Sheet2 tab **Sales**.
   b. Move the Inventory sheet so it comes after the Sales sheet.
   c. Change the tab color of the Inventory sheet to yellow (third column, fifth row).
   d. Change the tab color of the Sales sheet to aqua (fifth column, fourth row).
   e. Save the workbook.

5. **Preview and print a worksheet.**
   a. Make the Inventory sheet active.
   b. View it in Print Preview.
   c. Use the Zoom button to get a better look at your worksheet.
   d. Add your name to cell A11, then print one copy of the worksheet.

6. **Get Help.**
   a. Display the Office Assistant if it is not already displayed.
   b. Ask the Office Assistant for information about creating a formula.
   c. Print the information offered by the Office Assistant, using the Print button in the Help window.
   d. Close the Help window.

7. **Close a workbook and exit Excel.**
   a. Close the file using the Close command.
   b. If asked if you want to save the worksheet, click **No**.
   c. Exit Excel.

▶ Independent Challenge 1

The Excel Help feature provides definitions, explanations, procedures, and other helpful information. It also provides examples and demonstrations to show you how Excel features work. Topics include elements such as the active cell, status bar, buttons, and dialog boxes, as well as detailed information about Excel commands and options.

   a. Start Excel and open a new workbook using the New Workbook task pane.
   b. Click the **Office Assistant**; display it if necessary using the Show Office Assistant command on the Help menu.
   c. Type a question that will give you information about opening and saving a workbook. (*Hint*: You may have to ask the Office Assistant more than one question.)
   d. Print the information, close the Help window, then exit Excel.

▶ Independent Challenge 2

Spreadsheet software has many uses that can affect the way people work. The beginning of this unit discusses some examples of people using Excel. Use your own personal or business experiences to come up with five examples of how Excel could be used in a business setting.

   a. Start Excel.
   b. Write down five business tasks that you could complete more efficiently by using an Excel worksheet.
   c. Sketch a sample of each worksheet. See Table A-5, a sample payroll worksheet, as a guide.
   d. Open a new workbook and save it as **Sample Payroll** in the drive and folder where your Project Files are stored.

e. Give your worksheet a title in cell A1, then type your name in cell B1.

f. Enter the labels shown in Table A-5. Enter Hours Worked in column C and Hourly Wage in Column E.

g. Enter sample data for Hours Worked and Hourly Wage in the worksheet.

h. Save your work, then preview and print the worksheet.

i. Close the worksheet and exit Excel.

TABLE A-5: Sample payroll

Employee Name	Hours Worked	Hourly Wage
Dale Havorford		
Chris Wong		
Sharon Armenta		
Belinda Swanson		
Total		

▶ Independent Challenge 3

You are the office manager for Christine's Car Parts, a small auto parts supplier. Although the company is just three years old, it is expanding rapidly, and you are continually looking for ways to make your job easier. Last year you began using Excel to manage and maintain data on inventory and sales, which has greatly helped you to track information accurately and efficiently. The owner of the company has just approved your request to hire an assistant, who will be starting work in a week. You want to create a short training document that acquaints your new assistant with basic Excel skills.

a. Start Excel.

b. Create a new workbook and save it as **Training Workbook** in the drive and folder where your Project Files are located.

c. Enter a title for the worksheet in cell A1.

d. Make up and enter the values and labels for a sample spreadsheet. Make sure you have labels in column A.

e. Enter your name in cell D1.

f. Change the name of Sheet1 to Sample Data, then change the tab color of the Sample Data to another color.

g. Preview the worksheet, then print it.

h. Open a workbook based on a template from the Spreadsheet Solutions tab in the Templates dialog box. (You may need to insert your Office CD in order to do this.)

i. Save the workbook as **Template Sample**, then close the files and exit Excel.

e Independent Challenge 4

You can use the World Wide Web to help make informed purchasing decisions. Your supervisor has just given you approval for buying a new computer. While cost is not a limiting factor, you do need to provide a list of hardware and software requirements. You can use data found on the World Wide Web and use Excel to create a worksheet that details your purchase decision.

a. Connect to the Internet, then go to the CNET site at computers.com.

b. Use any of the links to locate information about the type of computer you want to purchase.

c. Locate data for the type of system you want using at least two vendors from within this site. When you find systems that meet your needs, print out the information. Be sure to identify each system's key features, such as the processor chip, hard drive capacity, RAM, and monitor size.

d. When you are finished gathering data, disconnect from the Internet.

e. Start Excel, open a new workbook and save it in the drive and folder where your Project Files are stored as **New Computer Data**.

f. Enter the manufacturers' names in columns and computer features (RAM, etc.) in rows. List the systems you found through your research, including the features you want (e.g., CD-ROM drive, etc.) and the cost for each system.

g. List the tax and shipping costs the manufacturer charges.

h. Indicate on the worksheet your final purchase decision by including descriptive text in a prominent cell. Enter your name in one of the cells.

i. Save, preview, and then print your worksheet.

j. Close the file and exit Excel.

▶ Visual Workshop

Create a worksheet similar to Figure A-22 using the skills you learned in this unit. Save the workbook as **Carrie's Camera and Darkroom** to the drive and folder where your Project Files are stored. Type your name in cell A11, then preview and print the worksheet.

FIGURE A-22

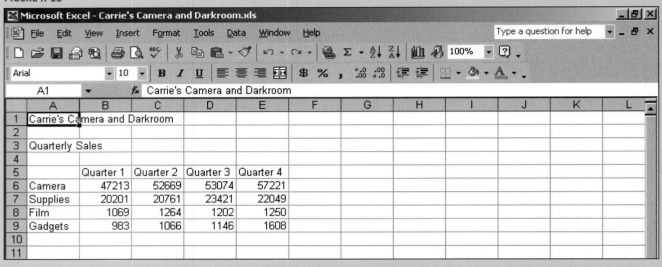

Building
and Editing Worksheets

Objectives

- ► **Plan and design a worksheet**
- [MOUS] ► **Edit cell entries**
- [MOUS] ► **Enter formulas**
- [MOUS] ► **Create complex formulas**
- [MOUS] ► **Introduce Excel functions**
- [MOUS] ► **Copy and move cell entries**
- [MOUS] ► **Understand relative and absolute cell references**
- [MOUS] ► **Copy formulas with relative cell references**
- [MOUS] ► **Copy formulas with absolute cell references**

Using your understanding of Excel basics, you can now plan and build your own worksheets. When you build a worksheet, you enter labels, values, and formulas into worksheet cells. Once you create a worksheet, you can save it in a workbook file and then print it. ✐ The MediaLoft marketing department has asked Jim Fernandez for an estimate of the average number of author appearances this summer. Marketing hopes that the number of appearances will increase 20% over last year's figures. Jim asks you to create a worksheet that summarizes appearances for last year and forecasts the summer appearances for this year.

Planning and Designing a Worksheet

Before you start entering data into a worksheet, you need to know the purpose and approximate layout of the worksheet.  To increase store traffic and sales, MediaLoft encourages authors to come to stores and sign their books. Jim wants to forecast MediaLoft's 2003 summer author appearances. The goal, already identified by the Marketing department, is to increase the year 2002 signings by 20%. Using the planning guidelines below, work with Jim as he plans this worksheet.

In planning and designing a worksheet it is important to:

► **Determine the purpose of the worksheet and give it a meaningful title**

Jim needs to forecast summer appearances for 2003. Jim titles the worksheet "Summer 2003 MediaLoft Author Events Forecast."

► **Determine your worksheet's desired results, or "output"**

Jim needs to begin scheduling author events and will use these forecasts to determine staffing and budget needs if the number of author events increases by 20%. He also wants to calculate the average number of author events because the Marketing department uses this information for corporate promotions.

► **Collect all the information, or "input," that will produce the results you want**

Jim gathers together the number of author events that occurred at four stores during the 2002 summer season, which runs from June through August.

► **Determine the calculations, or formulas, necessary to achieve the desired results**

First, Jim needs to total the number of events at each of the selected stores during each month of the summer of 2002. Then he needs to add these totals together to determine the grand total of summer appearances. Because he needs to determine the goal for the 2003 season, the 2002 monthly totals and grand total are multiplied by 1.2 to calculate the projected 20% increase for the 2003 summer season. He'll use the Average function to determine the average number of author appearances for the Marketing department.

► **Sketch on paper how you want the worksheet to look; identify where to place the labels and values**

Jim decides to put the store locations in rows and the months in columns. He enters the data in his sketch and notes the location of the monthly totals and the grand total. Below the totals, he writes out the formula for determining a 20% increase in 2002 appearances. He also includes a label for the average number of events calculations. Jim's sketch of his worksheet is shown in Figure B-1.

► **Create the worksheet**

Jim enters the labels first, to establish the structure of the worksheet. He then enters the values—the data summarizing the events—into his worksheet. Finally, he enters the formulas necessary to calculate totals, averages, and forecasts. These values and formulas will be used to calculate the necessary output. The worksheet Jim creates is shown in Figure B-2.

FIGURE B-1: Worksheet sketch showing labels, values, and calculations

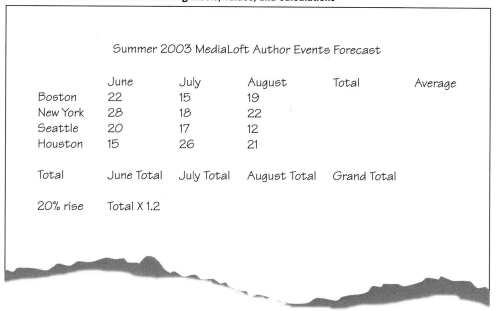

Summer 2003 MediaLoft Author Events Forecast

	June	July	August	Total	Average
Boston	22	15	19		
New York	28	18	22		
Seattle	20	17	12		
Houston	15	26	21		
Total	June Total	July Total	August Total	Grand Total	
20% rise	Total X 1.2				

FIGURE B-2: Jim's forecasting worksheet

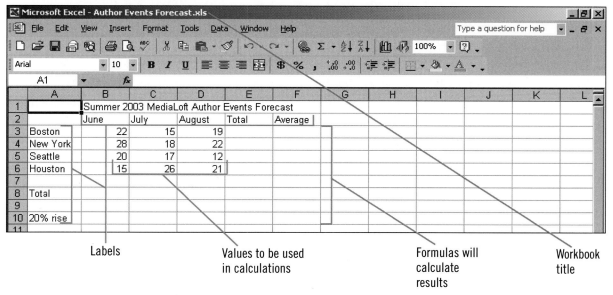

Labels

Values to be used in calculations

Formulas will calculate results

Workbook title

Excel 2002

Editing Cell Entries

You can change the contents of a cell at any time. To edit the contents of a cell, you first select the cell you want to edit. Then you have two options: you can click the formula bar or press [F2]. This puts Excel into Edit mode. Alternately, you can double-click any cell and start editing. To make sure you are in Edit mode, look at the **mode indicator** on the far-left side of the status bar. After planning and creating his worksheet, Jim notices that he entered the wrong value for the August Seattle events, and that Houston should replace San Diego. He asks you to edit these entries to correct them.

QuickTip

In the Open dialog box, you can double-click the file-name to open the workbook in one step.

1. Start Excel, open the workbook **EX B-1** from the drive and folder where your Project Files are stored, then save it as **Author Events Forecast**

2. Click cell **D5**
   This cell contains August events for the Seattle store, which you want to change to reflect the correct numbers.

3. Click to the right of **12** in the formula bar
   Excel goes into Edit mode, and the mode indicator on the status bar displays "Edit." A blinking vertical line called the **insertion point** appears in the formula bar, and if you move the mouse pointer to the formula bar, the pointer changes to Ⲓ, which is used for editing. See Figure B-3.

4. Press **[Backspace]**, type **8**, then click the **Enter button** 🗹 on the formula bar
   The value in cell D5 is changed from 12 to 18, and cell D5 remains selected.

5. Click cell **A6**, then press **[F2]**
   Excel returns to Edit mode, and the insertion point appears in the cell.

QuickTip

The Undo button 🔄 allows you to reverse up to 16 previous actions, one at a time.

6. Press **[Backspace]** nine times, type **Houston**, then press **[Enter]**
   The label changes to Houston, and cell A7 becomes the active cell. If you make a mistake, you can click the Cancel button ☒ on the formula bar *before* confirming the cell entry. If you notice the mistake *after* you have confirmed the cell entry, click the Undo button 🔄 on the Standard toolbar.

7. Double-click cell **C6**
   Double-clicking a cell also puts Excel into Edit mode with the insertion point in the cell.

8. Press **[Delete]** twice, then type **19**
   The number of book signings for July in Houston has been corrected. See Figure B-4.

9. Click 🗹 to confirm the entry, then click the **Save button** 💾 on the Standard toolbar

FIGURE B-3: **Worksheet in Edit mode**

Insertion point in formula bar

Edit mode indicator

Pointer used for editing

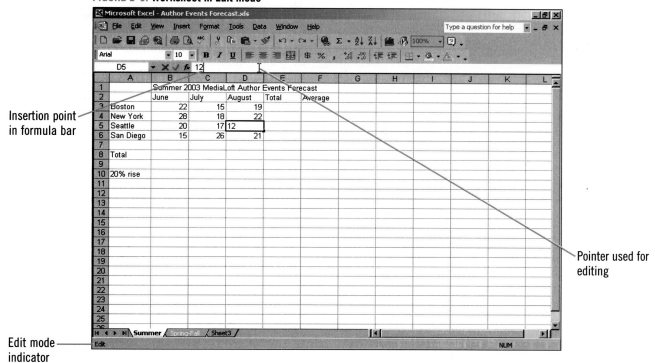

FIGURE B-4: **Edited worksheet**

Name box

Insertion point in cell

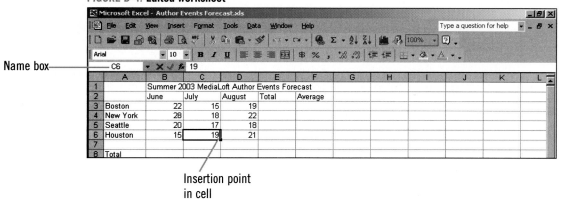

Recovering a lost workbook file

Sometimes while you are using Excel, you may experience a power failure or your computer may "freeze," making it impossible to continue working. If this type of interruption occurs, Excel has a built-in recovery feature that allows you to open and save files that were open at the time of the interruption. When you restart Excel after an interruption, the Document Recovery task pane opens on the left side of your screen displaying both original and recovered versions of the files that were open. If you're not sure which file to open (original or recovered), it's usually better to open the recovered file because it will have retained the latest information. You can, however, open and review all the versions of the file that were recovered and save the best one. Each file listed in the Document Recovery task pane has a list arrow with options that allow you to open the file, save the file, delete the file, or show repairs made to the file.

Entering Formulas

You use **formulas** to perform numeric calculations such as adding, multiplying, and averaging. Formulas in an Excel worksheet usually start with the equal sign (=), called the **formula prefix**, followed by cell addresses and range names. Arithmetic formulas use one or more **arithmetic operators** to perform calculations; see Table B-1. Using a cell address or range name in a formula is called **cell referencing**. If you change a value in a cell, any formula containing that cell reference will be automatically recalculated using the new value. ✎ Jim needs to total the values for the monthly author events for June, July, and August. He asks you to create formulas to perform these calculations.

Steps 1 2 3 4

1. Click cell **B8**
   This is the cell where you want to enter the calculation that totals the number of June events.

2. Type = (the equal sign)
   Placing an equal sign at the beginning of an entry tells Excel that a formula is about to be entered, rather than a label or a value. "Enter" appears on the status bar. The total number of June events is equal to the sum of the values in cells B3, B4, B5, and B6.

Trouble?

If you type an incorrect character, press [Backspace].

3. Type **b3+b4+b5+b6**
   Compare your worksheet to Figure B-5. Each cell address in the equation is shown in a matching color in the worksheet. For example, the cell address B3 is written in blue in the equation and is outlined in blue in the worksheet. This makes it easy to identify each cell in a formula.

Trouble?

If the formula instead of the result appears in the cell after you click ✓, make sure you began the formula with = (the equal sign).

4. Click the **Enter button** ✓ on the formula bar
   The result, 85, appears in cell B8. Cell B8 remains selected, and the formula appears in the formula bar. Excel is not case-sensitive: it doesn't matter if you type uppercase or lowercase characters when you enter cell addresses. Typing cell addresses is only one way of creating a formula. A more accurate method involves **pointing** at cells using the mouse, then using the keyboard to supply arithmetic operators.

5. Click cell **C8**, type =, click cell **C3**, type +, click cell **C4**, type +, click cell **C5**, type +, click cell **C6**, then click the **Enter button** ✓ on the formula bar
   When you clicked cell C3, a moving border surrounded the cell. This **moving border** indicates the cell used in the calculation. Moving borders can appear around a single cell or a range of cells. The total number of author appearances for July, 69, appears in cell C8. The pointing method of creating a formula is more accurate than typing, because it is easy to type a cell address incorrectly. Cell D8 also needs a total.

6. Click cell **D8**, type =, click cell **D3**, type +, click cell **D4**, type +, click cell **D5**, type +, click cell **D6**, then click the **Enter button** ✓ on the formula bar
   The total number of appearances for August, 80, appears in cell D8. Compare your worksheet to Figure B-6.

7. Click the **Save button** 🖫 on the Standard toolbar

FIGURE B-5: Worksheet showing cells in a formula

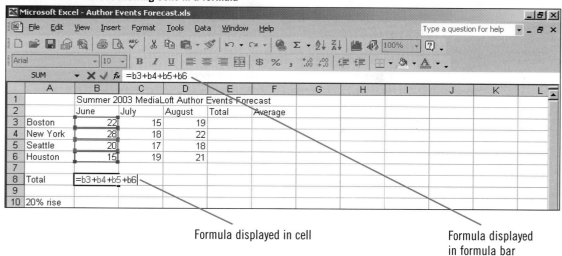

Formula displayed in cell

Formula displayed in formula bar

FIGURE B-6: Completed formulas

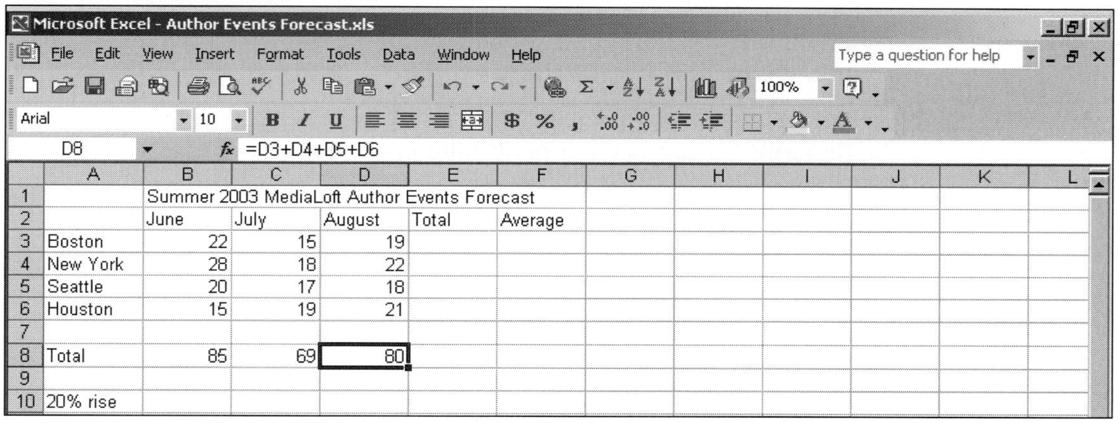

TABLE B-1: Excel arithmetic operators

operator	purpose	example
+	Addition	=A5+A7
–	Subtraction or negation	=A5–10
*	Multiplication	=A5*A7
/	Division	=A5/A7
%	Percent	=35%
^ (caret)	Exponent	=6^2 (same as 6^2)

Excel 2002

Creating Complex Formulas

The formula you entered is a simple formula containing one arithmetic operator, the plus sign. You can create a **complex formula**—an equation that uses more than one type of arithmetic operator. For example, you may need to create a formula that uses addition and multiplication. You can use arithmetic operators to separate tasks within a complex equation. In formulas containing more than one arithmetic operator, Excel uses the order of precedence rules to determine which operation to perform first. ◢ Jim wants you to total the values for the monthly author events for June, July, and August, and forecast what the 20% increase in appearances will be. You create a complex formula to perform these calculations.

Steps

1. Click cell **B10**, type =, click cell **B8**, then type *.2
   This part of the formula calculates 20% of the cell contents by multiplying the June total by .2 (or 20%). Because this part of the formula uses multiplication, it will be calculated first according to the rules of precedence.

QuickTip

Press [Esc] to turn off a moving border.

2. Type +, then click cell **B8**
   The second part of the formula adds the 20% increase to the original value of the cell. The mode indicator says Point, indicating you can add more cell references. Compare your worksheet to Figure B-7.

3. Click ✓ on the formula bar
   The result, 102, appears in cell B10.

4. Click cell **C10**, type =, click cell **C8**, type *.2, type +, click cell **C8**, then click ✓
   The result, 82.8, appears in cell C10.

5. Click cell **D10**, type =, click cell **D8**, type *.2, type +, click **D8**, then click ✓
   The result, 96, appears in cell D10. Compare your completed worksheet to Figure B-8.

6. Click the **Save button** 🖫 on the Standard toolbar

Editing formulas

You can edit formulas the same way you edit cell entries: you can click the cell containing the formula then edit it in the formula bar; you can also double-click a cell or press [F2] to enter Edit mode, and then edit the formula in the cell. After you are in Edit mode, use the arrow keys to move the insertion point left or right in the formula. Use [Backspace] or [Delete] to delete characters to the left or right of the insertion point, then type or point to new cell references or operators.

FIGURE B-7: Elements of a complex formula

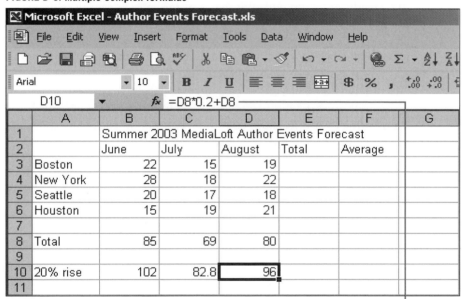

FIGURE B-8: Multiple complex formulas

Formula calculates a 20% increase over the value in cell D8 and displays the result in cell D10

CLUES TO USE

Order of precedence in Excel formulas

A formula can include several mathematical operations. When you work with formulas that have more than one operator, the order of precedence is very important. If a formula contains two or more operators, such as 4+.55/4000*25, the computer performs the calculations in a particular sequence based on these rules: Operations inside parentheses are calculated before any other operations. Exponents are calculated next, then any multiplication and division—from left to right.

Finally, addition and subtraction are calculated from left to right. In the example 4+.55/4000*25, Excel performs the arithmetic operations by first dividing 4000 into .55, then multiplying the result by 25, then adding 4. You can change the order of calculations by using parentheses. For example, in the formula (4+.55)/4000*25, Excel would first add 4 and .55, then divide that amount by 4000, then finally multiply by 25.

Introducing Excel Functions

Functions are predefined worksheet formulas that enable you to perform complex calculations easily. Like formulas, functions always begin with the formula prefix = (the equal sign). You can type functions, or you can use the Insert Function button to select the function you need from a list. The **AutoSum** button on the Standard toolbar enters the most frequently used function, SUM. A function can be used by itself within a cell, or as part of a formula. For example, to calculate monthly sales tax, you could create a formula that adds a range of cells (using the SUM function) and then multiplies the total by a decimal. ➤ Jim asks you to use the SUM function to calculate the grand totals in his worksheet and the AVERAGE function to calculate the average number of author events per store.

Steps

1. Click cell **E3**
   This is where you want the total of all Boston author events for June, July, and August.

2. Click the **AutoSum button** Σ on the Standard toolbar, then click the **Enter button** ✓ on the formula bar
   The formula =SUM(B3:D3) appears in the formula bar and the result, 56, appears in cell E3. By default, AutoSum adds the values in the cells above the cell pointer. If there are one or fewer values there, AutoSum adds the values to its left—in this case, the values in cells B3, C3, and D3. The information inside the parentheses is the **argument**, or the information Excel uses to calculate the function result. In this case, the argument is the range B3:D3.

3. Click cell **E4**, click Σ, then click ✓
   The total for the New York events appears in cell E4.

4. Click cell **E5**, then click Σ
   AutoSum sets up a function to add the two values in the cells above the active cell, but this time the default argument is not correct.

5. Click cell **B5** and hold down the mouse button, drag to cell **D5** to select the range **B5:D5**, then click ✓
   As you drag, the argument in the SUM function changes to reflect the selected range, and a yellow Argument ToolTip shows the function syntax. You can click any part of the ToolTip to display Help on the function.

6. Click cell **E6**, type **=SUM(**, click cell **B6** and drag to cell **D6**, click ✓, click cell **E8**, type **=SUM(**, click cell **B8** and drag to cell **D8**, click ✓, click cell **E10**, type **=SUM(**, click cell **B10** and drag to cell **D10**, then click ✓
   Compare your screen to Figure B-9. Excel adds the closing parenthesis.

7. Click cell **F3**, then click the **Insert Function button** ƒx on the formula bar
   The Insert Function dialog box and Wizard opens. Here you can select a function from a list. See Table B-2 for frequently used functions. The function you need to calculate averages—named AVERAGE—appears in the Most Recently Used function category.

8. Click **AVERAGE** in the Select a function list box, click **OK**; the Function Arguments dialog box opens; type **B3:D3** in the Number 1 text box, as shown in Figure B-10, then click **OK**

9. Click cell **F4**, click ƒx, verify that **AVERAGE** is selected, click **OK**, type **B4:D4**, click **OK**, click cell **F5**, click ƒx, click **AVERAGE**, click **OK**, type **B5:D5**, click **OK**, click cell **F6**, click ƒx, click **AVERAGE**, click **OK**, type **B6:D6**, then click **OK**
   The result for Boston (cell F3) is 18.66667; the result for New York (cell F4) is 22.66667; the result for Seattle (cell F5) is 18.33333; and the result for Houston (cell F6) is 18.33333, giving you the averages for all four stores.

10. Enter your name in cell **A25**, click the **Save button** 🖫 on the Standard toolbar, then click the **Print button** 🖨 on the Standard toolbar

FIGURE B-9: Worksheet with SUM functions entered

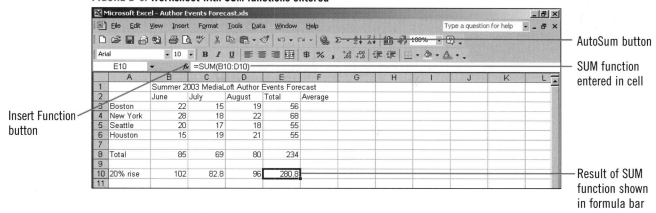

Insert Function button

AutoSum button

SUM function entered in cell

Result of SUM function shown in formula bar

FIGURE B-10: Using Insert Function to create a formula

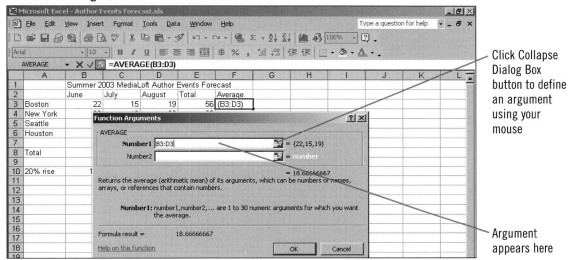

Click Collapse Dialog Box button to define an argument using your mouse

Argument appears here

TABLE B-2: Frequently used functions

function	description
SUM (*argument*)	Calculates the sum of the arguments
AVERAGE (*argument*)	Calculates the average of the arguments
MAX (*argument*)	Displays the largest value among the arguments
MIN (*argument*)	Displays the smallest value among the arguments
COUNT (*argument*)	Calculates the number of values in the arguments

Using the MIN and MAX functions

Other commonly used functions include MIN and MAX. You use the MIN function to calculate the minimum, or smallest, value in a selected range; the MAX function calculates the maximum, or largest, value in a selected range. The MAX function is included in the Most Recently Used function category in the Insert Function dialog box, while both the MIN and MAX function can be found in the Statistical category. These functions are particularly useful in larger worksheets.

Copying and Moving Cell Entries

Excel 2002

Using the Cut, Copy, and Paste buttons or the Excel drag-and-drop feature, you can copy or move information from one cell or range in your worksheet to another. When you cut or move information, the original data does not remain in the original location. You can also cut, copy, and paste labels and values from one worksheet to another. ✐ Jim needs to include the 2003 forecast for spring and fall author events. He's already entered the spring data and will finish entering the labels and data for the fall. He asks you to copy information from the spring report to the fall report.

Steps ₁₂₃⁴

1. **Click the Spring-Fall sheet tab of the Author Events Forecast workbook**
   The store names in cells A6:A7 are incorrect.

2. **Click the Summer sheet tab, select the range A5:A6, then click the Copy button** on the Standard toolbar
   The selected range (A5:A6) is copied to the **Office Clipboard**, a temporary storage area that holds the selected information you copy or cut. A moving border surrounds the selected range until you press [Esc] or copy additional information to the Clipboard. The information you copied remains in the selected range.

Trouble?
If the Clipboard task pane does not open, click Edit on the menu bar, then click Office Clipboard.

3. **Click the Spring-Fall sheet tab, select the range A6:A7, click the Paste button** on the Standard toolbar, select the range **A4:A9**, then click
   The Clipboard task pane opens when you copy a selection to the already-occupied Clipboard. You can use the Clipboard task pane to copy, cut, store, and paste up to 24 items. Each item in the pane displays its contents.

QuickTip
After you paste an item, the Paste Options button appears. If you move the pointer over it, the Paste Options list arrow appears, letting you choose whether to paste the contents or only the formatting.

4. **Click cell A13, click** [Boston New York Seattle Houston Total] **in the Clipboard Task Pane to paste the contents in cell A13, then click the Close button** ✖ **in the Task Pane title bar to close it**
   The item is copied into the range A13:A18. When pasting an item from the Clipboard into the worksheet, you only need to specify the top-left cell of the range where you want to paste the selection. The Total label in column E is missing from the fall forecast.

5. **Click cell E3, position the pointer on any edge of the cell until the pointer changes to** ⟲ **, then press and hold down [Ctrl]**
   The pointer changes to the copy pointer ⟲⁺.

6. **While still pressing [Ctrl], press and hold the left mouse button, drag the cell contents to cell E12, release the mouse button, then release [Ctrl]**
   This **drag-and-drop technique** is useful for copying cell contents. As you dragged, an outline of the cell moved with the pointer, as shown in Figure B-11, and a ScreenTip appeared tracking the current position of the item as you moved it. When you released the mouse button, the Total label appeared in cell E12. You can also use drag and drop to move data to a new cell.

Trouble?
When you use drag and drop to move data into occupied cells, Excel asks if you want to replace the existing cells. Click OK to replace the contents with those of the cell you are moving.

7. **Click cell C1, position the pointer on the edge of the cell until it changes to** ⟲ **, then drag the cell contents to A1**
   You don't use [Ctrl] when moving information with drag and drop. You can easily enter the fall events data into the range B13:D16.

8. **Using the information shown in Figure B-12, enter the author events data for the fall into the range B13:D16**

9. **Click the Save button** 💾 **on the Standard toolbar**

FIGURE B-11: Using drag-and-drop to copy information

Copy button

Paste button

Copied cell

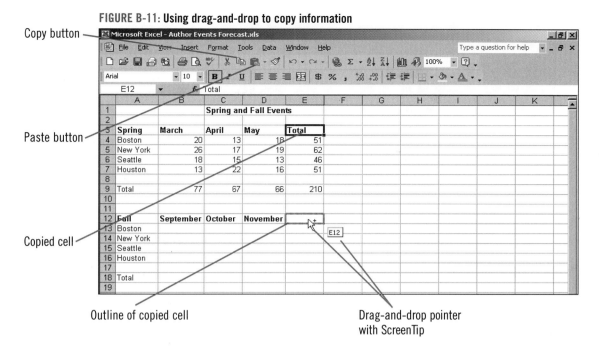

Outline of copied cell

Drag-and-drop pointer with ScreenTip

FIGURE B-12: Worksheet with fall author event data entered

	Fall	September	October	November	Total
10					
11					
12	Fall	September	October	November	Total
13	Boston	22	17	20	
14	New York	27	16	24	
15	Seattle	19	19	18	
16	Houston	15	25	18	
17					
18	Total				
19					
20					
21					
22					
23					
24					
25					

Summer / Spring-Fall / Sheet3

Ready   Sum=240

Sum of selected range appears in status bar

CLUES TO USE

Using the Office Clipboard

The Office Clipboard, shown in the task pane in Figure B-13, lets you copy and paste multiple items such as text, images, tables, or Excel ranges within or between Microsoft Office applications. The Office Clipboard can hold up to 24 items copied or cut from any Office program. The Clipboard task pane displays the items stored on the Office Clipboard. You choose whether to delete the first item from the Clipboard when you copy the 25th item. The collected items remain in the Office Clipboard and are available to you until you close all open Office programs. You can specify when and where to show the Office Clipboard task pane by clicking the options list arrow at the bottom of the Clipboard pane.

FIGURE B-13: Office Clipboard task pane

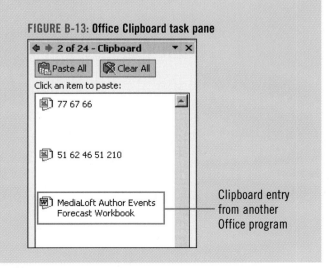

Clipboard entry from another Office program

Understanding Relative and Absolute Cell References

As you work in Excel, you will often want to reuse formulas in different parts of the worksheet. This will save you time because you won't have to retype them. For example, you may want to perform a what-if analysis showing one set of sales figures using a lower forecast in one part of the worksheet and another set using a higher forecast in another area. But when you copy formulas, it is important make sure that they refer to the correct cells. To do this, you need to understand relative and absolute cell references. ◄████ Jim often reuses formulas in different parts of his worksheets to examine different possible outcomes, so he wants you to understand relative and absolute cell references.

► **Use relative references when cell relationships remain unchanged.**

When you create a formula that references other cells, Excel normally does not "record" the exact cell references, but instead the relationship to the cell containing the formula. For example, in Figure B-14, cell E5 contains the formula: =SUM(B5:D5). When Excel retrieves values to calculate the formula in cell E5, it actually looks for "the cell three columns to the left of the formula, which in this case is cell B5", "the cell two columns to the left of the formula" and so on. This way, if you copy the cell to a new location such as cell E6, the results will reflect the new formula location, and will automatically retrieve the values in cells B6, C6, and D6. This is called **relative cell referencing**, because Excel is recording the input cells *in relation to* the formula cell.

In most cases, you will use relative cell references, which is the Excel default. In Figure B-14, the formulas in E5:E9 and in B9:E9 contain relative cell references. They total the "three cells to the left of" or the "four cells above" the formulas.

► **Use absolute cell references when one relationship changes.**

There are times when you want Excel to retrieve formula information from a specific cell, and you don't want that cell to change when you copy the formula to a new location. For example, you might have a price in a specific cell that you want to use in all formulas, regardless of their location. If you used relative cell referencing, the formula results would be incorrect, because Excel would use a different cell every time you copied the formula. Therefore you need to use an **absolute cell reference**, a reference that does not change when you copy the formula.

You create an absolute cell reference by placing a $ (dollar sign) before both the column letter and the row number for the cell's address, using the [F4] function key on the keyboard. Figure B-15 displays the formulas used in Figure B-14. The formulas in cells B15 to D18 use absolute cell references to refer to a potential sales increase of 50%, shown in cell B12.

FIGURE B-14: Location of relative references

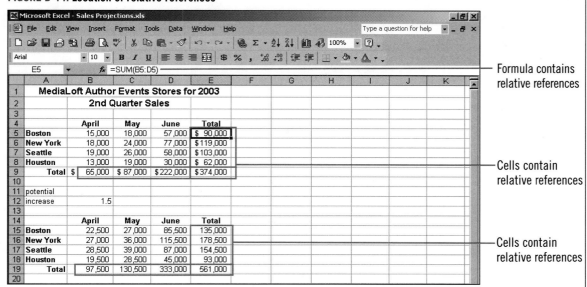

Formula contains relative references

Cells contain relative references

Cells contain relative references

FIGURE B-15: Absolute and relative reference formulas

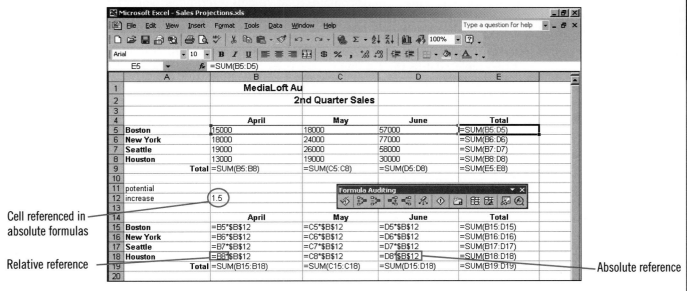

Cell referenced in absolute formulas

Relative reference

Absolute reference

CLUES TO USE

Using a mixed reference

Sometimes when you copy a formula, you'll want to change the row reference but keep the column reference the same. This type of cell referencing combines elements of both absolute and relative referencing and is called a mixed reference. When copied, the mixed reference C$14 changes the column relative to its new location but prevents the row from changing.

In the mixed reference $C14, the column would not change but the row would be updated relative to its location. Like the absolute reference, a mixed reference can be created using the [F4] function key. With each press of the [F4] key, you cycle through all the possible combinations of relative, absolute, and mixed references ($C$14, C$14, $C14, C14).

Excel 2002

Copying Formulas with Relative Cell References

Copying and moving formulas allows you to reuse formulas you've already created. Copying formulas, rather than retyping them, is faster and helps to prevent typing errors. You can use the Copy and Paste commands or the Fill Right method to copy formulas. ✐ Jim wants you to copy the formulas that total the appearances by region and by month from the spring to the fall.

Steps 1234

1. **Click cell E4, then click the Copy button** 📋 **on the Standard toolbar**
   The formula for calculating the total number of spring Boston author events is copied to the Clipboard. Notice that the formula =SUM(B4:D4) appears in the formula bar.

QuickTip

To specify components of the copied cell or range prior to pasting, click Edit on the menu bar, then click Paste Special. You can selectively copy formulas, values, comments, validation, and formatting attributes, and specify calculations, as well as transpose cells or paste the contents as a link.

2. **Click cell E13, then click the Paste button** 📋 **on the Standard toolbar**
   The formula from cell E4 is copied into cell E13, where the new result of 59 appears. Notice in the formula bar that the cell references have changed, so that the range B13:D13 appears in the formula. This formula contains **relative cell references**, which tell Excel to copy the formula to a new cell, but to substitute new cell references so that the relationship of the cells to the formula in its new location remains unchanged. In this case, Excel adjusted the formula so that cells D13, C13, and B13—the three cell references immediately to the left of E13—replaced cells D4, C4, and B4, the three cell references to the left of E4. Notice that the bottom-right corner of the active cell contains a small square, called the **fill handle**. You can use the fill handle to copy labels, formulas, and values. This option is called **AutoFill**.

3. **Position the pointer over the fill handle until it changes to ✛, press and hold the left mouse button, then drag the fill handle to select the range E13:E16**
   See Figure B-16.

4. **Release the mouse button**
   A formula similar to the one in cell E13 now appears in the range E14:E16. Again, because the formula uses relative cell references, cells E14 through E16 correctly display the totals for the fall author events. After you release the mouse button, the **AutoFill Options button** appears. If you move the pointer over it and click its list arrow, you can specify what you want to fill and whether or not you want to include formatting.

5. **Click cell B9, click Edit on the menu bar, then click Copy**

Trouble?

If the Clipboard task pane opens, click the Close button. If the Office Assistant appears, right-click it, then click Hide.

6. **Click cell B18, click Edit on the menu bar, then click Paste**
   See Figure B-17. The formula for calculating the September events appears in the formula bar. You also need totals to appear in cells C18, D18, and E18. You could use the fill handle again, but another option is to use a menu command.

7. **Select the range B18:E18**

8. **Click Edit on the menu bar, point to Fill, then click Right**
   The rest of the totals are filled in correctly. Compare your worksheet to Figure B-18.

9. **Click the Save button** 📋 **on the Standard toolbar**

FIGURE B-16: Using the fill handle

12	Fall	September	October	November	Total	
13	Boston	22	17	20	59	Formula in cell E13 will be copied to E14:E16
14	New York	27	16	24		
15	Seattle	19	19	18		Fill handle
16	Houston	15	25	18		
17						Mouse pointer
18	Total					

FIGURE B-17: Copied formula

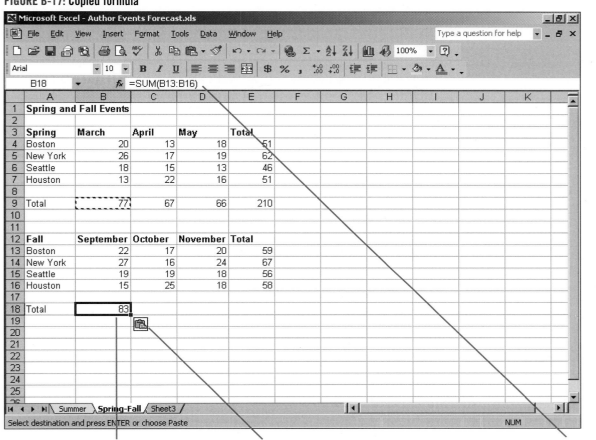

Copied formula result   Paste Options button   Copied formula cell references

FIGURE B-18: Completed worksheet with all formulas copied

12	Fall	September	October	November	Total
13	Boston	22	17	20	59
14	New York	27	16	24	67
15	Seattle	19	19	18	56
16	Houston	15	25	18	58
17					
18	Total	83	77	80	240

CLUES TO USE

Filling cells with sequential text or values

Often, you'll need to fill cells with sequential text: months of the year, days of the week, years, or text plus a number (Quarter 1, Quarter 2, . . .). You can easily fill cells using sequences by dragging the fill handle. As you drag the fill handle, Excel automatically extends the existing sequence. (The contents of the last filled cell appear in the ScreenTip.) Use the Fill Series command on the Edit menu to examine all of the available fill series options.

Excel 2002

Copying Formulas with Absolute Cell References

When copying formulas, you might want a cell reference to always refer to a particular cell address. In such an instance, you would use an absolute cell reference. An **absolute cell reference** always refers to a specific cell address when the formula is copied. You create an absolute reference by placing a dollar sign ($) before the row letter and column number of the address (for example $A$1). ✒️ The staff in the Marketing department hopes the number of author events will increase by 20% over last year's figures. Jim wants you to add a column that calculates a possible increase in the number of spring events in 2003. He asks you to do a what-if analysis and recalculate the spreadsheet several times, changing the percentage by which the number of appearances might increase each time.

Steps 1 2 3 4

1. Click cell **G1**, type **Change**, then press [➡]

   You can store the increase factor that will be used in the what-if analysis in cell H1.

2. Type **1.1**, then press **[Enter]**

   The value in cell H1 represents a 10% increase in author events.

3. Click cell **G3**, type **What if?**, then press **[Enter]**

4. Click cell **G4**, type **=**, click **E4**, type *****, click **H1**, then click the **Enter button** ☑ on the formula bar

   The result, 56.1, appears in cell G4. This value represents the total spring events for Boston if there is a 10% increase. Jim wants to perform a what-if analysis for all the stores.

QuickTip

Before you copy or move a formula, check to see if you need to use an absolute cell reference.

5. Drag the fill handle to extend the selection from **G4** to **G7**

   The resulting values in the range G5:G7 are all zeros. When you copy the formula it adjusts so that the formula in cell G5 is =E5*H2. Because there is no value in cell H2, the result is 0, an error. You need to use an absolute reference in the formula to keep the formula from adjusting itself. That way, it will always reference cell H1. You can change the relative cell reference to an absolute cell reference by using [F4].

6. Click cell **G4**, press **[F2]** to change to Edit mode, then press **[F4]**

   When you press [F2], the **range finder** outlines the equation's arguments in blue and green. When you press [F4], dollar signs appear, changing the H1 cell reference to an absolute reference. See Figure B-19.

7. Click ☑ on the formula bar, then drag the fill handle to extend the selection to range **G5:G7**

   The formula correctly contains an absolute cell reference, and the value of G4 remains unchanged at 56.1. The correct values for a 10% increase appear in cells G4:G7. You complete the what-if analysis by changing the value in cell H1 to indicate a 25% increase in events.

8. Click cell **H1**, type **1.25**, then click ☑

   The values in the range G4:G7 change to reflect the 25% increase. Compare your completed worksheets to Figure B-20. Because events only occur in whole numbers, the numbers' appearance can be changed later.

9. Enter your name in cell **A25**, click the **Save button** 💾 on the Standard toolbar, click the **Print button** 🖨 on the Standard toolbar, close the workbook, then exit Excel

FIGURE B-19: Absolute cell reference in cell G4

	Microsoft Excel - Author Events Forecast.xls											

Absolute cell references in formula

Incorrect values due to relative references in copied formulas

	A	B	C	D	E	F	G	H	I	J	K
1	Spring and Fall Events						Change	1.1			
2											
3	Spring	March	April	May	Total		What if?				
4	Boston	20	13	18	51		=E4*$H$1				
5	New York	26	17	19	62		0				
6	Seattle	18	15	13	46		0				
7	Houston	13	22	16	51		0				
8											
9	Total	77	67	66	210						

AVERAGE ▼ ✕ ✓ ƒₓ =E4*$H$1

FIGURE B-20: Completed worksheets

Summer 2003 MediaLoft Author Events Forecast

	June	July	August	Total	Average
Boston	22	15	19	56	18.66667
New York	28	18	22	68	22.66667
Seattle	20	17	18	55	18.33333
Houston	15	19	21	55	18.33333
Total	85	69	80	234	
20% rise	102	82.8	96	280.8	

Spring and Fall Events   Change   1.25

Spring	March	April	May	Total	What if?
Boston	20	13	18	51	63.75
New York	26	17	19	62	77.5
Seattle	18	15	13	46	57.5
Houston	13	22	16	51	63.75
Total	77	67	66	210	

Fall	September	October	November	Total
Boston	22	17	20	59
New York	27	16	24	67
Seattle	19	19	18	56
Houston	15	25	18	58
Total	83	77	80	240

Inserting and deleting selected cells

As you add formulas to your workbook, you may need to insert or delete cells, not entire rows or columns. When you do this, Excel automatically adjusts cell references to reflect their new locations. To insert cells, click Insert on the menu bar, then click Cells. The Insert dialog box opens, asking if you want to insert a cell and move the selected cell down or to the right of the new one. To delete one or more selected cells, click Edit on the menu bar, click Delete, and, in the Delete dialog box, indicate which way you want to move the adjacent cells. When using this option, be careful not to disturb row or column alignment that may be necessary to make sense of the worksheet.

Practice

▶ Concepts Review

Label each element of the Excel worksheet window shown in Figure B-21.

FIGURE B-21

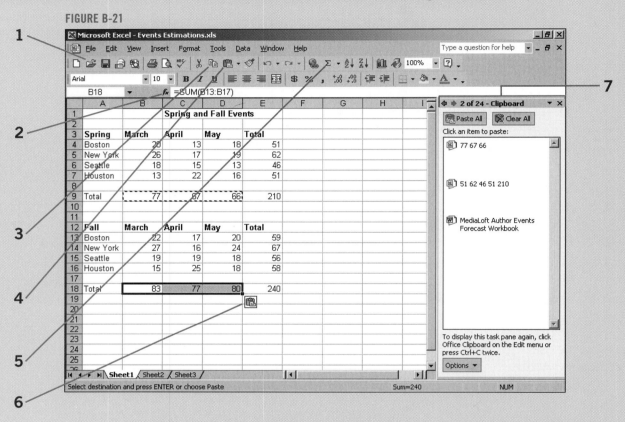

Match the term or button with the statement that describes it.

8. **Fill handle**
9. **Function**
10.
11.
12. **Formula**

a. A predefined formula that provides a shortcut for commonly used calculations
b. A cell entry that performs a calculation in an Excel worksheet
c. Used to copy labels, formulas, and values
d. Adds the selected range to the Office Clipboard.
e. Used to paste cells

Select the best answer from the list of choices.

13. **What type of cell reference changes when it is copied?**
    a. Absolute
    b. Circular
    c. Looping
    d. Relative

14. **What character is used to make a reference absolute?**
    a. &
    b. ^
    c. $
    d. @

15. **Which button is used to enter data in a cell?**

a.   c. ▣

b. ✖   d. ✓

► Skills Review

1. **Edit cell entries and work with ranges.**
   a. Start Excel, open the workbook EX B-2 from the drive and folder where your Project Files are stored then save it as **Office Furnishings**.
   b. Change the quantity of Tables to **27**.
   c. Change the price of Desks to **285**.
   d. Change the quantity of Easels to **18**.
   e. Enter your name in cell A40, then save the workbook.

2. **Enter formulas.**
   a. In cell B6, use the pointing method to enter the formula **B2+B3+B4+B5**.
   b. In cell D2, use the pointing method to enter the formula **B2*C2**.
   c. Save your work.

3. **Create complex formulas.**
   a. In cell B8, enter the formula **(B2+B3+B4+B5)/4**.
   b. In cell C8, enter the formula **(C2+C3+C4+C5)/4**.
   c. Save your work.

4. **Introduce Excel functions.**
   a. Enter the label **Min Price** in cell A9.
   b. In cell C9, enter the function **MIN(C2:C5)**.
   c. Enter the label **Max Price** in cell A10.
   d. Create a formula in cell C10 that determines the maximum price.
   e. Save your work.

5. **Copy and move cell entries.**
   a. Select the range **A1:C6**, then copy the range to cell A12.
   b. Select the range **D1:E1**, then use drag and drop to copy the range to cell D12.
   c. Move the contents of cell G1 to cell E9, then save your work.

6. **Copy formulas with relative cell references.**
   a. Copy the formula in D2 into cells D3:D5.
   b. Copy the formula in D2 into cells D13:D16.
   c. Save the worksheet.

7. **Copy formulas with absolute cell references.**
   a. In cell E10, enter the value **1.375**.
   b. In cell E2, create a formula containing an absolute reference that multiplies D2 and E10.
   c. Use the fill handle to copy the formula in E2 into cells **E3:E5**.
   d. Use the copy and paste buttons to copy the formula in E2 into cells **E13:E16**.
   e. Delete cells A13:E13, shifting the cells up, then edit the formula in cell B16 so the missing reference is removed.
   f. Change the amount in cell E10 to **2.873**.
   g. Select cells A1:E1 and insert cells, shifting cells down.
   h. Enter **Inventory Estimate** in cell A1.
   i. Save, preview, print, and close the workbook, then exit Excel.

Independent Challenge 1

You are the box office manager for the Young Brazilians Jazz Band, a popular new group. Your responsibilities include tracking seasonal ticket sales for the band's concerts and anticipating ticket sales for the next season. The group sells four types of tickets: reserved, general, senior, and student tickets.

The 2003–2004 season includes five scheduled concerts: Spring, Summer, Fall, Winter, and Thaw. You will plan and build a worksheet that tracks the sales of each of the four ticket types for all five concerts.

FIGURE B-22

	A	B	C	D	E	F	G	H
1			2003-2004 Season					
2			Young Brazilians Jazz Band					Increase
3								1.05
4		Reserved	General	Senior	Student			
5	Concerts	Seating	Admission	Citizens	Tickets	Totals		What if?
6	Spring	285	50	30	20	385		404.25
7	Summer	135	25	35	20	215		225.75
8	Fall	130	50	25	20	225		236.25
9	Winter	160	100	30	20	310		325.5
10	Thaw	250	60	35	20	365		383.25
11	Total	960	285	155	100	1500		1575
12								

   a. Think about the results you want to see, the information you need to build into these worksheets, and what types of calculations must be performed.

   b. Sketch sample worksheets on a piece of paper to indicate how the information should be laid out. What information should go in the columns? In the rows?

   c. Start Excel, open a new workbook, then save it as **Young Brazilians** in the drive and folder where your Project Files are stored.

   d. Plan and build a worksheet that tracks the sales of each of the four ticket types for all five concerts. Build the worksheets by entering a title, row labels, column headings, and formulas.

   e. Enter your own sales data. No concert sold more than 400 tickets, and the Reserved category was the most popular.

   f. Calculate the total ticket sales for each concert, the total sales for each of the four ticket types, and the total sales for all tickets.

   g. Name the worksheet **Sales Data** and color the tab Red.

   h. Copy the Sales Data worksheet to a blank worksheet, name the copied worksheet **5% Increase**, and color the tab aqua.

   i. Modify the 5% increase sheet so that a 5% increase in sales of all ticket types is shown in a separate column. See Figure B-22 for a sample worksheet.

   j. Enter your name in a worksheet cell.

   k. Save your work, preview and print the worksheets, then close the workbook and exit Excel.

Independent Challenge 2

The Beautiful You Salon is a small but growing beauty salon that has hired you to organize its accounting records using Excel. The owners want you to track its expenses using Excel. Before you were hired, one of the bookkeepers entered last year's expenses in a workbook, but the analysis was never completed.

   a. Start Excel, open the workbook EX B-3 then save it as **Beautiful You Finances** in the drive and folder where your Project Files are stored. The worksheet includes labels for functions such as the Average, Maximum, and Minimum amounts of each of the expenses in the worksheet.

   b. Think about what information would be important for the bookkeeping staff to know.

   c. Create your sketch using the existing worksheet as a foundation.

   d. Create formulas in the Total column and row using the AutoSum function.

   e. Create formulas in the Average, Maximum, and Minimum columns and rows using the appropriate functions, dragging to select the range.

   f. Rename Sheet1 **Expenses** and add a color to the tab.

   g. Enter your name in a worksheet cell.

   h. Save your work, preview and print the worksheet, then close the workbook and exit Excel.

► Independent Challenge 3

You have been promoted to computer lab manager at Learn-It-All, a local computer training center. It is your responsibility to make sure there are enough computers for students during scheduled classes. Currently, you have five classrooms: four with IBM PCs and one with Macintoshes. Classes are scheduled Monday, Wednesday, and Friday in two-hour increments from 9 a.m. to 5 p.m. (the lab closes at 7 p.m.), and each room can currently accommodate 30 computers.

You plan and build a worksheet that tracks the number of students who can currently use the available computers per room. You create your enrollment data. Using an additional worksheet, you show the impact of an enrollment increase of 25%.

    a. Think about how to construct these worksheets to create the desired output.

    b. Sketch sample paper worksheets to indicate how the information should be laid out.

    c. Start Excel, open a new workbook, then save it as **Learn-it-All** in the drive and folder where your Project Files are stored.

    d. Create a worksheet by entering a title, row labels, column headings, data, and formulas. Name the sheet to easily identify its contents.

    e. Create a second sheet by copying the information from the initial sheet.

    f. Name the second sheet to easily identify its contents.

    g. Add color to each sheet tab.

    h. Enter your name in a cell in each sheet.

    i. Save your work, preview and print each worksheet, then close the workbook and exit Excel.

Independent Challenge 4

Your company is opening a branch office in Great Britain and your boss is a fanatic about keeping the thermostats at a constant temperature during each season of the year. Because she grew up in the U.S., she is only familiar with Fahrenheit temperatures and doesn't know how to convert them to Celsius. She has asked you to find out the Celsius equivalents for the thermostatic settings she wants to use. She prefers the temperature to be 65 degrees F in the winter, 62 degrees F in the spring, 75 degrees in the summer, and 70 degrees F in the fall. You can use the Web and Excel to determine the new settings.

    a. Start Excel, open a new workbook, then save it as **Temperature Conversions** in the drive and folder where your Project Files are stored.

    b. Go to the Alta Vista search engine at www.altavista.com and enter search text such as "temperature conversions". You can also use Yahoo!, Excite, Infoseek, or another search engine of your choice. Locate a site that tells you how to convert Fahrenheit temperatures to Celsius. (*Hint*: One possible site you can use to determine these conversions is http://home.clara.net/brianp/, then click on the Temperature link.)

    c. Think about how to create an Excel equation that will perform the conversion.

    d. Create column and row titles using Table B-3 to get started.

    e. In the appropriate cell, create an equation that calculates the conversion of a Fahrenheit temperature to a Celsius temperature.

    f. Copy the equation, then paste it in the remaining Celsius cells.

    g. Enter your name in a worksheet cell.

    h. Save and print your work.

TABLE B-3

Temperature Conversions

Season	Fahrenheit	Celsius
Spring	62	
Winter	68	
Summer	75	
Fall	70	

▶ Visual Workshop

Create a worksheet similar to Figure B-23 using the skills you learned in this unit. Save the workbook as **Annual Budget** in the drive and folder where your Project Files are stored. Enter your name in cell A13, then preview and print the worksheet.

FIGURE B-23

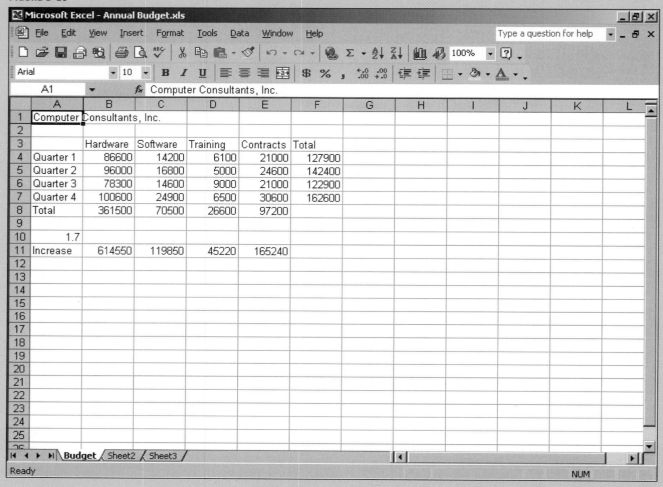

Formatting

a Worksheet

Objectives

- ⌐MOUS⌐ ▶ **Format values**
- ⌐MOUS⌐ ▶ **Use fonts and font sizes**
- ⌐MOUS⌐ ▶ **Change attributes and alignment**
- ⌐MOUS⌐ ▶ **Adjust column widths**
- ⌐MOUS⌐ ▶ **Insert and delete rows and columns**
- ⌐MOUS⌐ ▶ **Apply colors, patterns, and borders**
- ⌐MOUS⌐ ▶ **Use conditional formatting**
- ⌐MOUS⌐ ▶ **Check spelling**

You can use Excel formatting features to make a worksheet more attractive, to make it easier to read, or to emphasize key data. You do this by using different colors and fonts for the cell contents, adjusting column and row widths, and inserting and deleting columns and rows. The marketing managers at MediaLoft have asked Jim Fernandez to create a workbook that lists advertising expenses for all MediaLoft stores. Jim has prepared a worksheet for the New York City store containing this information, which he can adapt later for use in other stores. He asks you to use formatting to make the worksheet easier to read and to call attention to important data.

Excel 2002

Formatting Values

If you enter a value in a cell and you don't like the way the data appears, you can adjust the cell's format. **Formatting** determines how labels and values appear in cells, such as boldface, italic, with or without dollar signs or commas, and the like. Formatting changes only the way a value or label appears; it does not alter cell data in any way. To format a cell, first select it, then apply the formatting. You can format cells and ranges before or after you enter data. ▰▰▰ The Marketing department has requested that Jim begin by listing the New York City store's advertising expenses. Jim developed a worksheet that lists advertising invoices. He entered all the information and now wants you to format some of the labels and values. Because some of the changes might also affect column widths, you make all formatting changes before widening the columns.

Steps

QuickTip

Recall that to save a workbook in a different location, you click File on the menu bar, click Save As, click the Save in list arrow and navigate to a new drive or folder, type a new filename if necessary, then click Save.

1. **Start Excel, open the Project File EX C-1 from the drive and folder where your Project Files are stored, then save it as Ad Expenses**

   The store advertising worksheet appears in Figure C-1. You can display numeric data in a variety of ways, such as with decimals or leading dollar signs. Excel provides a special format for currency, which adds two decimal places and a dollar sign.

2. **Select the range E4:E32, then click the Currency Style button 🖫 on the Formatting toolbar**

   Excel adds dollar signs and two decimal places to the Cost data. Excel automatically resizes the column to display the new formatting. Another way to format dollar values is to use the comma format, which does not include the $ sign.

QuickTip

Select any range of contiguous cells by clicking the top-left cell, pressing and holding [Shift], then clicking the bottom-right cell. Add a row to the selected range by continuing to hold down [Shift] and pressing [↓], add a column by pressing [→].

3. **Select the range G4:I32, then click the Comma Style button 🖫 on the Formatting toolbar**

   The values in columns G, H, and I display the comma format. You can also format percentages by using the Formatting toolbar.

4. **Select the range J4:J32, click the Percent Style button 🖫 on the Formatting toolbar, then click the Increase Decimal button 🖫 on the Formatting toolbar to show one decimal place**

   The % of Total column is now formatted with a percent sign (%) and one decimal place. You decide that you prefer the percentages rounded to the nearest whole number.

5. **Click the Decrease Decimal button 🖫**

   You can also apply a variety of formats to dates in a worksheet.

6. **Select the range B4:B31, click Format on the menu bar, click Cells, then if necessary click the Number tab**

   The Format Cells dialog box opens with the Number tab in front and the Date category already selected. See Figure C-2.

7. **Select the format 14-Mar-01 in the Type list box, then click OK**

   The dates in column B appear in the format you selected. You decide you don't need the year to appear in the Inv. Due column.

QuickTip

The 3-14-01 format displays a single-digit day (such as 5/9/03) just as 9-May-03 does. The format below it displays the same day as 5/09/03.

8. **Select the range C4:C31, click Format on the menu bar, click Cells, click 14-Mar in the Type list box, then click OK**

   Compare your worksheet to Figure C-3.

9. **Click the Save button 🖫 on the Standard toolbar**

FIGURE C-1: Advertising expense worksheet

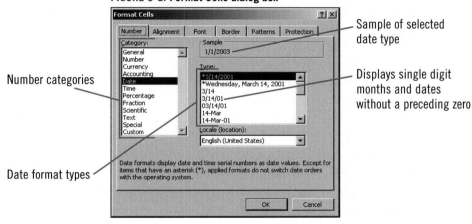

FIGURE C-2: Format Cells dialog box

Sample of selected date type

Number categories

Date format types

Displays single digit months and dates without a preceding zero

FIGURE C-3: Worksheet with formatted values

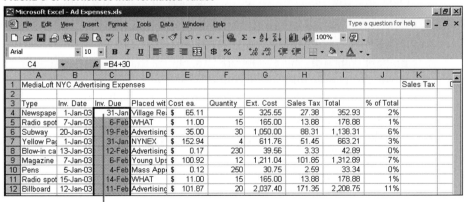

Date formats appear without year

Using the Format Painter

You can "paint" a cell's format into other cells by using the Format Painter button 🖌 on the Standard toolbar. This is similar to using copy and paste to copy information, but instead of copying cell contents, you copy only the cell format. Select the cell containing the desired format, then click 🖌. The pointer changes to ⊕🖌. Use this pointer to select the cell or range you want to contain the new format. You can paint a cell's format onto multiple cells by double-clicking 🖌, then clicking each cell that you want to paint with ⊕🖌. When you are finished painting formats, you can turn off the Format Painter by pressing [Esc] or by clicking 🖌 again.

Using Fonts and Font Sizes

A **font** is the name for a collection of characters (letters, numerals, symbols, and punctuation marks) with a similar, specific design. The **font size** is the physical size of the text, measured in units called points. A **point** is equal to 1/72 of an inch. The default font in Excel is 10-point Arial. You can change the font, the size, or both of any worksheet entry or section by using the Format command on the menu bar or by using the Formatting toolbar. Table C-1 shows several fonts in different sizes. Now that the data is formatted, Jim wants you to change the font and size of the labels and the worksheet title so that they stand out more from the data.

Steps

1. Press **[Ctrl][Home]** to select cell A1

2. Click **Format** on the menu bar, click **Cells**, then click the **Font tab** in the Format Cells dialog box
   See Figure C-4.

3. Scroll down the **Font list** to see an alphabetical listing of the fonts available on your computer, click **Times New Roman** in the Font list box, click **24** in the Size list box, then click **OK**
   The title font appears in 24-point Times New Roman, and the Formatting toolbar displays the new font and size information. You can also change a font and increase the font size by using the Formatting toolbar. The column headings should stand out more from the data.

4. Select the range **A3:J3**, then click the **Font list arrow** [Arial ▾] on the Formatting toolbar
   Notice that the fonts on this font list actually look like the font they represent.

5. Click **Times New Roman** in the Font list, click the **Font Size** list arrow [10 ▾], then click **14** in the Font Size list
   Compare your worksheet to Figure C-5. Notice that some of the column headings are now too wide to appear fully in the column. Excel does not automatically adjust column widths to accommodate cell formatting; you have to adjust column widths manually. You'll learn to do this in a later lesson.

6. Click the **Save button** 🖫 on the Standard toolbar

TABLE C-1: Types of fonts

font	12 point	24 point	font	12 point	24 point
Arial	Excel	Excel	Playbill	Excel	Excel
Comic Sans MS	Excel	Excel	Times New Roman	Excel	Excel

FIGURE C-4: Font tab in the Format Cells dialog box

Currently selected font

Available fonts may differ on your computer

Effects options

Type a custom font size or select from the list

Font style options

Sample of selected font and formatting

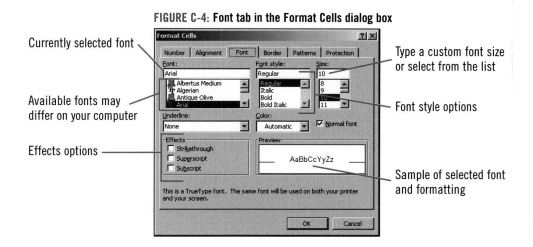

FIGURE C-5: Worksheet with formatted title and labels

Font and size of active cell or range

Column headings now 14-point Times New Roman

Title after changing to 24-point Times New Roman

CLUES TO USE

Inserting Clip Art

You can add clips to your worksheets to make them look more professional. A clip is an individual media file, such as art, sound, animation, or a movie. Clip art refers to images such as a corporate logo, a picture, or a photo; Excel comes with many clips that you can use. To add clip art to your worksheet, click Insert on the menu bar, point to Picture, then click Clip Art. The Insert Clip Art task pane appears. Here you can search for clips by typing one or more keywords (words related to your subject) in the Search text box, then clicking Search. Clips that relate to your keywords appear in the Clip Art task pane, as shown in Figure C-6. Click the image you want. (If you have a standard Office installation and have a dial-up Internet connection, you will have fewer images available.) You can also add your own images to a worksheet by clicking Insert on the menu bar, pointing to Picture, then clicking From File. Navigate to the file you want, then click Insert. To resize an image, drag its lower right corner. To move an image, drag it to a new location.

FIGURE C-6: Results of search on keyword "magic"

Changing Attributes and Alignment

Excel 2002

Attributes are styling formats such as bold, italics, and underlining that you can apply to affect the way text and numbers look in a worksheet. You can also change the **alignment** of labels and values in cells to be left, right, or center. You can apply attributes and alignment options from the Formatting toolbar or from the Alignment tab of the Format Cells dialog box. See Table C-2 for a list and description of the available attribute and alignment toolbar buttons. ✐ Now that you have applied new fonts and font sizes to his worksheet labels, Jim wants you to further enhance the worksheet's appearance by adding bold and underline formatting and centering some of the labels.

Steps

1. Press **[Ctrl][Home]** to move to cell A1, then click the **Bold button** 🅱 on the Formatting toolbar
   The title appears in bold.

2. Select the range **A3:J3**, then click the **Underline button** 🅤 on the Formatting toolbar
   Excel underlines the text in the column headings in the selected range.

QuickTip

Overuse of any attribute can be distracting and make a workbook less readable. Be consistent, adding emphasis the same way throughout.

3. Click cell **A3**, click the **Italics button** 🅸 on the Formatting toolbar, then click 🅱
   The word "Type" appears in boldface italic type. Notice that the Bold, Italics, and Underline buttons are selected.

4. Click 🅸
   Excel removes italics from cell A3 but the bold and underline formatting attributes remain.

QuickTip

Use formatting shortcuts on any selected range: [Ctrl][B] to bold, [Ctrl][I] to italicize, and [Ctrl][U] to underline.

5. Select the range **B3:J3**, then click 🅱
   Bold formatting is added to the rest of the labels in the column headings. The title would look better if it were centered over the data columns.

6. Select the range **A1:J1**, then click the **Merge and Center button** 🖽 on the Formatting toolbar
   The Merge and Center button creates one cell out of the 10 cells across the row, then centers the text in that newly created large cell. The title "MediaLoft NYC Advertising Expenses" is centered across the 10 columns you selected. You can change the alignment within individual cells using toolbar buttons; you can split merged cells into their original components by selecting the merged cells, then clicking 🖽.

QuickTip

To clear all formatting, click Edit on the menu bar, point to Clear, then click Formats.

7. Select the range **A3:J3**, then click the **Center button** 🖽 on the Formatting toolbar
   Compare your screen to Figure C-7. Although they may be difficult to read, notice that all the headings are centered within their cells.

8. Click the **Save button** 💾 on the Standard toolbar

Rotating and indenting cell entries

In addition to applying fonts and formatting attributes, you can rotate or indent cell data within a cell to further change its appearance. You can rotate text within a cell by altering its alignment. To change alignment, select the cells you want to modify, click Format on the menu bar, click Cells, then click the Alignment tab. Click a position in the Orientation box, or type a number in the degrees text box to change from the default horizontal alignment, then click OK. You can indent cell contents using the Increase Indent button 📇 on the Formatting toolbar, which moves cell contents to the right one space, or the Decrease Indent button 📇, which moves cell contents to the left one space.

FIGURE C-7: Worksheet with formatting attributes applied

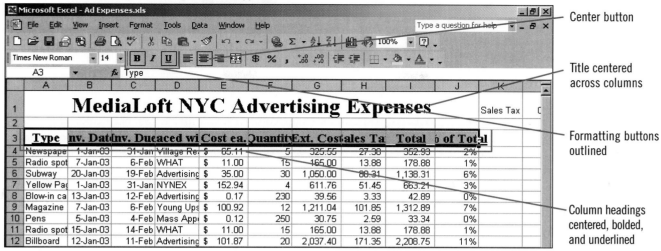

Center button

Title centered across columns

Formatting buttons outlined

Column headings centered, bolded, and underlined

TABLE C-2: Attribute and Alignment buttons on the Formatting toolbar

button	description	button	description
B	Bolds text	☰	Aligns text on the left side of the cell
I	Italicizes text	☰	Centers text horizontally within the cell
U	Underlines text	☰	Aligns text on the right side of the cell
▦	Adds lines or borders	▦	Centers text across columns, and combines two or more selected adjacent cells into one cell

Using AutoFormat

Excel has 17 predefined worksheet formats to make formatting easier and to give you the option of consistently styling your worksheets. AutoFormats are designed for worksheets with labels in the left column and top rows, and totals in the bottom row or right column. To use AutoFormat, select the data to be formatted—or place your mouse pointer anywhere within the range to be selected (Excel can automatically detect a range of cells)—click Format on the menu bar, click AutoFormat, select a format from the sample boxes, as shown in Figure C-8, then click OK.

FIGURE C-8: AutoFormat dialog box

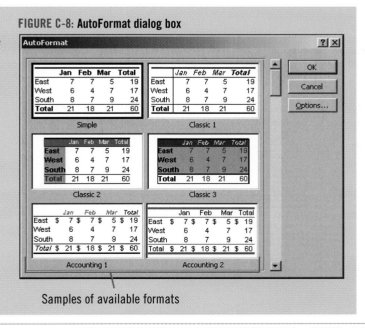

Samples of available formats

Adjusting Column Widths

As you continue formatting a worksheet, you might need to adjust column widths to accommodate a larger font size or style. The default column width is 8.43 characters wide, a little less than one inch. With Excel, you can adjust the column width for one or more columns by using the mouse or the Column command on the Format menu. Table C-3 describes the commands available on the Format Column menu. ✐ Jim notices that some of the labels in column A have been truncated and don't fit in the cells. He asks you to adjust the widths of the columns so that the labels appear in their entirety.

Steps 1234

1. Position the pointer on the line between the column A and column B headings
The **column heading** is the gray box at the top of each column containing a letter. The pointer changes to ↔, as shown in Figure C-9. You position the pointer on the right edge of the column that you are adjusting. The Yellow Pages entries are the widest in the column.

2. Click and drag the ↔ pointer to the right until the column displays the Yellow Pages entries fully
The **AutoFit** feature lets you use the mouse to resize a column so it automatically accommodates the widest entry in a cell.

> **QuickTip**
> To reset columns to the default width, click the column headings to select the columns, click Format on the menu bar, point to Column, click Standard Width, then click OK.

3. Position the pointer on the column line between columns B and C headings until it changes to ↔, then double-click
Column B automatically widens to fit the widest entry, in this case, the column label.

4. Use AutoFit to resize columns C, D, and J
You can also use the Column Width command on the Format menu to adjust several columns to the same width.

5. Select the range F5:I5
Columns can be adjusted by selecting any cell in the column.

6. Click Format on the menu bar, point to Column, then click Width
The Column Width dialog box appears. Move the dialog box, if necessary, by dragging it by its title bar so you can see the selected columns. The column width measurement is based on the number of characters in the Normal font (in this case, Arial).

> **Trouble?**
> If "######" appears after you adjust a column of values, the column is too narrow to display the contents. Increase the column width until the values appear.

7. Type 11 in the Column Width text box, then click OK
The column widths change to reflect the new setting. See Figure C-10.

8. Click the Save button 🖫 on the Standard toolbar

TABLE C-3: Format Column commands

command	description	command	description
Width	Sets the width to a specific number of characters	Unhide	Unhide(s) column(s)
AutoFit Selection	Fits to the widest entry	Standard Width	Resets width to default widths
Hide	Hide(s) column(s)		

FIGURE C-9: Preparing to change the column width

Resize pointer between columns A and B

Row 2 heading

Column D heading

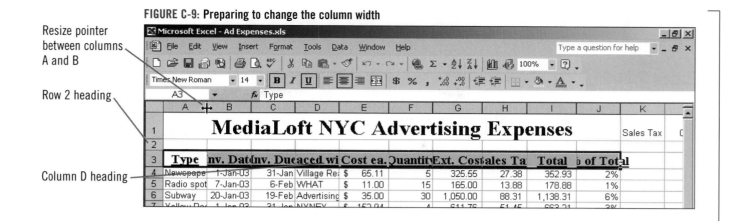

FIGURE C-10: Worksheet with column widths adjusted

Columns widened to display text

Columns widened to same width

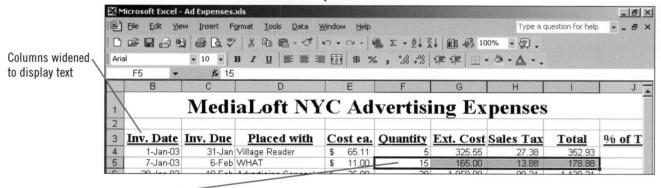

Specifying row height

The Row Height command on the Format menu allows you to customize row height to improve readability. Row height is calculated in points, the same units of measure used for fonts. The row height must exceed the size of the font you are using. Normally, you don't need to adjust row heights manually. If you format something in a row to be a larger point size, Excel will adjust the row to fit the largest point size in the row. You can also adjust row height by placing the **┿** pointer under the row heading and dragging to the desired height.

Inserting and Deleting Rows and Columns

As you modify a worksheet, you might find it necessary to insert or delete rows and columns to keep your worksheet current. For example, you might need to insert rows to accommodate new inventory products or remove a column of yearly totals that are no longer necessary. ▶ Jim has already improved the appearance of his worksheet by formatting the labels and values in the worksheet. Now he decides to improve the overall appearance of the worksheet by inserting a row between the last row of data and the totals. Jim has located a row of inaccurate data and an unnecessary column that he wants you to delete.

Steps 1 2 3 4

1. **Right-click cell A32, then click Insert**
   The Insert dialog box opens. See Figure C-11. You can choose to insert a column or a row, or you can shift the data in the cells in the active column right or in the active row down. An additional row between the last row of data and the totals will visually separate the totals.

> **QuickTip**
>
> Inserting or deleting rows or columns can cause problems in formulas that contain absolute cell references. After adding rows or columns to a worksheet, be sure to proof your formulas.

2. **Click the Entire row option button, then click OK**
   A blank row appears between the totals and the Billboard data. Excel inserts rows above the cell pointer and inserts columns to the left of the cell pointer. When you insert a new row, the contents of the worksheet shift down from the newly inserted row. The formula result in cell E33 has not changed. When you insert a new column, the contents of the worksheet shift to the right from the point of the new column. To insert a single row, you can also right-click the row heading immediately below where you want the new row, then click Insert. To insert multiple rows, drag across row headings to select the same number of rows as you want to insert. The Insert Options button 🖌 appears beside cell A33. When you place ▷ over 🖌, you can click the list arrow and select from the following options: Format Same As Above, Format same As Below, or Clear Formatting.

3. **Click the row 27 heading**
   Hats from Mass Appeal Inc. will no longer be part of the advertising campaign. All of row 27 is selected, as shown in Figure C-12.

> **QuickTip**
>
> Use the Edit menu, or right-click the selected row and click Delete, to remove a selected row. Pressing [Delete] removes the contents of a selected row; the row itself remains.

4. **Click Edit in the menu bar, then click Delete**
   Excel deletes row 27, and all rows below this shift up one row.

5. **Click the column J heading**
   The percentage information is calculated elsewhere and is no longer necessary in this worksheet.

6. **Click Edit in the menu bar, then click Delete**
   Excel deletes column J. The remaining columns to the right shift left one column.

7. **Click the Save button 🖫 on the Standard toolbar**

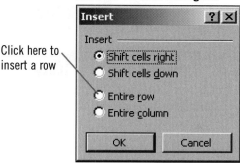

FIGURE C-11: Insert dialog box

Click here to insert a row

FIGURE C-12: Worksheet with row 27 selected

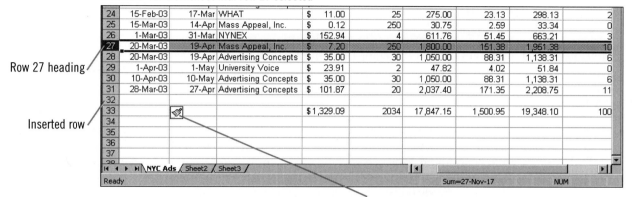

24	15-Feb-03	17-Mar	WHAT	$	11.00	25	275.00	23.13	298.13	2
25	15-Mar-03	14-Apr	Mass Appeal, Inc.	$	0.12	250	30.75	2.59	33.34	0
26	1-Mar-03	31-Mar	NYNEX	$	152.94	4	611.76	51.45	663.21	3
27	20-Mar-03	19-Apr	Mass Appeal, Inc.	$	7.20	250	1,800.00	151.38	1,951.38	10
28	20-Mar-03	19-Apr	Advertising Concepts	$	35.00	30	1,050.00	88.31	1,138.31	6
29	1-Apr-03	1-May	University Voice	$	23.91	2	47.82	4.02	51.84	0
30	10-Apr-03	10-May	Advertising Concepts	$	35.00	30	1,050.00	88.31	1,138.31	6
31	28-Mar-03	27-Apr	Advertising Concepts	$	101.87	20	2,037.40	171.35	2,208.75	11
32										
33					$1,329.09	2034	17,847.15	1,500.95	19,348.10	100
34										
35										
36										
37										

Row 27 heading

Inserted row

NYC Ads / Sheet2 / Sheet3 /

Ready   Sum=27-Nov-17   NUM

Insert Options button may appear in a
different location, or may not be visible

Excel 2002

CLUES TO USE

Adding and editing comments

Much of your Excel work may be in collaboration with teammates with whom you share worksheets. You can share ideas with other worksheet users by adding comments within selected cells. To include a comment in a worksheet, click the cell where you want to place the comment, click Insert on the menu bar, then click Comment. A resizable text box containing the computer's user name opens where you can type your comments. A small, red triangle appears in the upper-right corner of a cell containing a comment. If the comments are not already displayed, workbook users can point to the triangle to display the comment. To see all worksheet comments, as shown in Figure C-13, click View on the menu bar, then click Comments. To edit a comment click the cell containing the comment, click Insert on the menu bar, then click Edit Comment. To delete a comment, right-click the cell containing the comment, then click Delete Comment.

FIGURE C-13: Comments in worksheet

20	Subway	22-Feb-03	24-Mar	Advertising Concepts	$	35.00
21	Radio spot	1-Feb-03	3-Mar	WHAT	$	11.00
22	Newspaper	25-Feb-03	27-Mar	Village Reader	$	65.11
23	Blow-in cards	10-Mar-03	9-Apr	**Jim Fernandez:**	$	0.17
24	Radio spot	15-Feb-03	17-Mar	Should we continue with	$	11.00
25	Pens	15-Mar-03	14-Apr	these ads, or expand to	$	0.12
26	Yellow Pages	1-Mar-03	31-Mar	other publications?	$	152.94
27	Subway	20-Mar-03	19-Apr	Advertising Concepts	$	35.00
28	Newspaper	1-Apr-03	1-May	**Jim Fernandez:**	$	23.91
29	Subway	10-Apr-03	10-May	We need to evaluate	$	35.00
30	Billboard	28-Mar-03	27-Apr	whether we should	$	101.87
31				continue these ads.		
32					$1,321.89
33					
34					

NYC Ads / Sheet2 / Sheet3 /

Ready

Applying Colors, Patterns, and Borders

You can use colors, patterns, and borders to enhance the overall appearance of a worksheet and to make it easier to read. You can add these enhancements by using the Patterns or Borders tabs in the Format Cells dialog box or by using the Borders and Color buttons on the Formatting toolbar. You can apply color or patterns to the background of a cell, to a range, or to cell contents. You can also apply borders to all the cells in a worksheet or only to selected cells to call attention to individual or groups of cells. See Table C-4 for a list of border buttons and their functions. Jim asks you to add a pattern, a border, and color to the title of the worksheet to give it a more professional appearance.

Steps

1. Press **[Ctrl][Home]** to select cell **A1**, then click the **Fill Color list arrow** on the Formatting toolbar
The color palette appears.

> **QuickTip**
>
> Use color sparingly. Too much color can divert the reader's attention from the worksheet data.

2. Click the **Turquoise** color (fourth row, fifth column)
Cell A1 has a turquoise background, as shown in Figure C-14. Cell A1 spans columns A through I because of the Merge and Center command used for the title.

3. Click **Format** on the menu bar, then click **Cells**
The Format Cells dialog box opens.

4. Click the **Patterns tab** if it is not already displayed
See Figure C-15. A high contrast between foreground and background increases the readability of cell contents.

5. Click the **Pattern list arrow**, click the **Thin Diagonal Crosshatch pattern** (third row, last column), then click **OK**
A border also enhances a cell's appearance. Unlike underlining, which is a text formatting tool, borders extend the width of the cell.

> **QuickTip**
>
> You can also draw cell borders using the mouse pointer. Click the Borders list arrow on the Formatting toolbar. Click Draw Borders, then drag to create borders or boxes.

6. Click the **Borders list arrow** on the Formatting toolbar, then click the **Thick Bottom Border** (second row, second column) on the Borders palette
It can be difficult to view a border in a selected cell.

7. Click cell **A3**
The border is a nice enhancement. Font color can also help distinguish information in a worksheet.

> **QuickTip**
>
> The default color on the Fill Color and Font Color buttons changes to the last color you selected.

8. Select the range **A3:I3**, click the **Font Color list arrow** on the Formatting toolbar, then click **Blue** (second row, third column from the right) on the palette
The text changes color, as shown in Figure C-16.

9. Click the **Print Preview button** on the Standard toolbar, preview the first page, click **Next** to preview the second page, click **Close** on the Print Preview toolbar, then click the **Save button** on the Standard toolbar

FIGURE C-14: **Background color added to cell**

Cell A1 with turquoise background

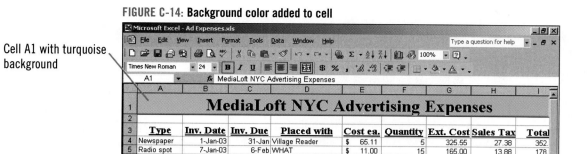

FIGURE C-15: **Patterns tab in the Format Cells dialog box**

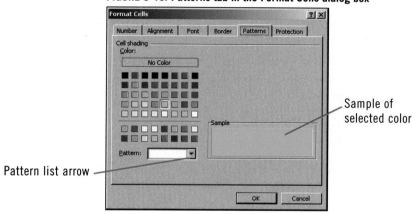

Sample of selected color

Pattern list arrow

FIGURE C-16: **Worksheet with colors, patterns, and border**

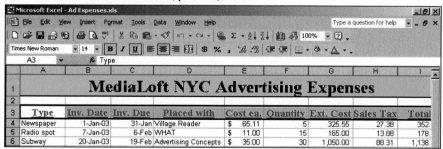

TABLE C-4: **Border buttons**

button	function	button	function	button	function
	No Border		Bottom Double Border		Top and Thick Bottom Border
	Bottom Border		Thick Bottom Border		All Borders
	Left Border		Top and Bottom Border		Outside Borders
	Right Border		Top and Double Bottom Border		Thick Box Border

Excel 2002

Using Conditional Formatting

Formatting makes worksheets look professional and helps distinguish different types of data. You can have Excel automatically apply formatting depending on specific outcomes in cells. You might, for example, want advertising costs above a certain number to appear in red boldface and lower values to appear in blue. Automatically applying formatting attributes based on cell values is called **conditional formatting**. If the data meets your criteria, Excel applies the formats you specify. ✐ Jim wants the worksheet to include conditional formatting so that total advertising costs greater than $175 appear in boldface red type. He asks you to create the conditional format in the first cell in the Total cost column.

Steps 1 2 3 4

1. Click cell **G4**
   Use the scroll bars if necessary, to make column G visible.

2. Click **Format** on the menu bar, then click **Conditional Formatting**
   The Conditional Formatting dialog box opens. Depending on the logical operator you've selected (such as "greater than" or "not equal to"), the Conditional Formatting dialog box displays different input boxes. You can define up to three different conditions that let you determine the outcome, and then assign formatting attributes to each one. You define the condition first. The default setting for the first condition is "Cell Value Is" "between."

Trouble?
If the Office Assistant appears, close it by clicking the No, don't provide help now button.

3. To change the current condition, click the **Operator list arrow**, then click **greater than or equal to**
   Because you changed the operator from "between," which required text boxes for two values, only one value text box now appears. The first condition is that the cell value must be greater than or equal to some value. See Table C-5 for a list of options. The value can be a constant, formula, cell reference, or date. That value is set in the third box.

4. Click the **Value text box**, then type **175**
   Now that you have assigned the value, you need to specify what formatting you want for cells that meet this condition.

5. Click **Format**, click the **Color list arrow**, click **Red** (third row, first column), click **Bold** in the Font style list box, click **OK**, compare your settings to Figure C-17, then click **OK** to close the Conditional Formatting dialog box
   The value in cell G4, 325.55, is formatted in bold red numbers because it is greater than 175, meeting the condition to apply the format. You can copy conditional formats the same way you would copy other formats.

6. With cell G4 selected, click the **Format Painter button** 🖌 on the Standard toolbar, then drag ⊕🖌 to select the range **G5:G30**

7. Click cell **G4**
   Compare your results to Figure C-18. All cells with values greater than or equal to 175 in column G appear in bold red text.

8. Press **[Ctrl][Home]** to move to cell A1

9. Click the **Save button** 💾 on the Standard toolbar

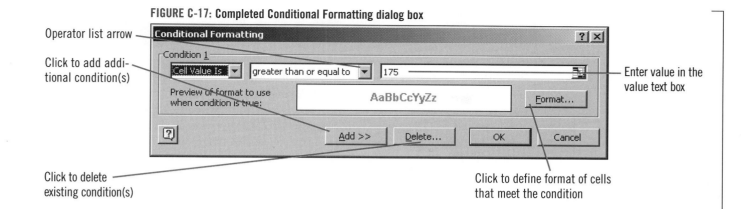

FIGURE C-17: Completed Conditional Formatting dialog box

Operator list arrow

Click to add additional condition(s)

Enter value in the value text box

Click to delete existing condition(s)

Click to define format of cells that meet the condition

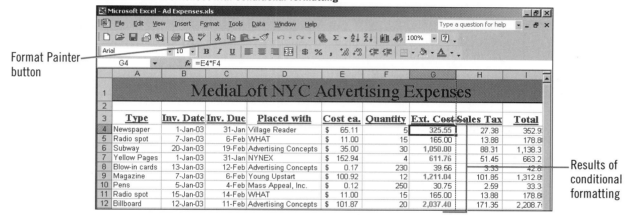

FIGURE C-18: Worksheet with conditional formatting

Format Painter button

Results of conditional formatting

TABLE C-5: Conditional formatting options

option	mathematical equivalent	option	mathematical equivalent
Between	$X>Y<Z$	Greater than	$Z>Y$
Not between	$B\not>C\not<A$	Less than	$Y<Z$
Equal to	$A=B$	Greater than or equal to	$A\geq B$
Not equal to	$A\neq B$	Less than or equal to	$Z\leq Y$

CLUES TO USE

Deleting conditional formatting

Because it's likely that the conditions you define will change, you can delete any conditional format you define. Select the cell(s) containing conditional formatting, click Format on the menu bar, click Conditional Formatting, then click Delete. The Delete Conditional Format dialog box opens, as shown in Figure C-19. Select the check boxes for any of the conditions you want to delete, click OK, then click OK again. The previously assigned formatting is deleted—leaving the cell's contents intact.

FIGURE C-19: Delete Conditional Format dialog box

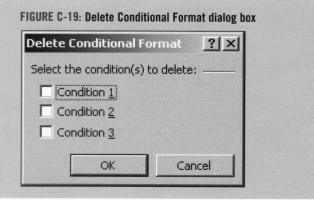

Excel 2002

Checking Spelling

A single misspelled word can cast doubt on the validity and professional value of your entire workbook. Excel includes a spelling checker to help you ensure workbook accuracy. The spelling checker scans your worksheet, displays words it doesn't find in its built-in dictionary, and when possible suggests replacements. To check other sheets in a multiple-sheet workbook, you need to display each sheet and run the spelling checker again. Because the built-in dictionary cannot possibly include all the words that each of us needs, you can add words to the dictionary, such as your company name, an acronym, or an unusual technical term. The spelling checker will no longer consider that word misspelled. Any words you've added to the dictionary using Word, Access, or PowerPoint are also available in Excel. Because he will distribute this workbook to the marketing managers, Jim asks you to check its spelling.

Steps

Trouble?

If a language other than English is being used, the Spelling English dialog box will list the name of that language.

1. **Click the Spelling button on the Standard toolbar**
   The Spelling English (U.S.) dialog box opens, as shown in Figure C-21, with MediaLoft selected as the first misspelled word in the worksheet. For any word you have the option to Ignore or Ignore All cases the spell checker flags, or Add the word to the dictionary.

2. **Click Ignore All for MediaLoft**
   The spell checker found the word "cards" misspelled and offers "crabs" as an alternative.

3. **Scroll through the Suggestions list, click cards, then click Change**
   The word "Concepts" is also misspelled and the spell checker suggests the correct spelling.

4. **Click Change**
   When no more incorrect words are found, Excel displays a message indicating that all the words on that worksheet have been checked.

5. **Click OK**

6. **Enter your name in cell A34, then press [Ctrl][Home]**

QuickTip

You can set the Excel AutoCorrect feature to correct spelling as you type. Click Tools on the menu bar, then click AutoCorrect Options.

7. **Click the Save button on the Standard toolbar, then preview the worksheet**

8. **In the Preview window, click Setup, under Scaling click Fit to option button to print the worksheet on one page, click OK, click Print, then click OK**
   Compare your printout to Figure C-22.

9. **Click File on the menu bar, then click Exit to close the workbook without saving changes and exit Excel**

Using e-mail to send a workbook

You can use e-mail to send an entire workbook from within Excel. To send a workbook as an e-mail message attachment, open the workbook, click File, point to Send to, then click Mail Recipient (as Attachment). You supply the To and (optional) Cc information, as shown in Figure C-20, then click Send. You can also route a workbook to one or more recipients on a routing list. Click File, point to Send to, then click Routing Recipient. Click Create New Contact and enter contact information, then fill in the Routing slip. Depending on your e-mail program and Web browser, you may have to follow a different procedure.

FIGURE C-20: E-mailing an Excel workbook

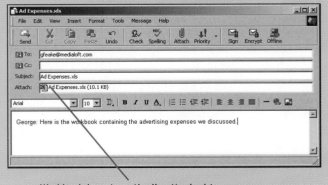

Workbook is automatically attached to message

FIGURE C-21: Spelling English dialog box

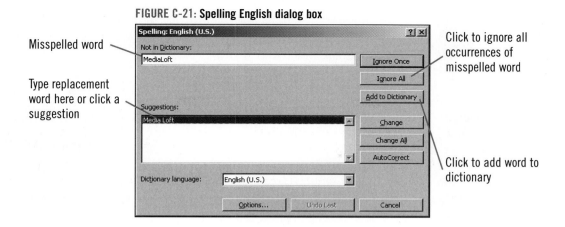

Misspelled word

Type replacement word here or click a suggestion

Click to ignore all occurrences of misspelled word

Click to add word to dictionary

FIGURE C-22: Completed worksheet

MediaLoft NYC Advertising Expenses

Sales Tax   0.0841

Type	Inv. Date	Inv. Due	Placed with	Cost ea.	Quantity	Ext. Cost	Sales Tax	Total
Newspaper	1-Jan-03	31-Jan	Village Reader	$ 65.11	5	325.55	27.38	352.93
Radio spot	7-Jan-03	6-Feb	WHAT	$ 11.00	15	165.00	13.88	178.88
Subway	20-Jan-03	19-Feb	Advertising Concepts	$ 35.00	30	1,050.00	88.31	1,138.31
Yellow Pages	1-Jan-03	31-Jan	NYNEX	$ 152.94	4	611.76	51.45	663.21
Blow-in cards	13-Jan-03	12-Feb	Advertising Concepts	$ 0.17	230	39.56	3.33	42.89
Magazine	7-Jan-03	6-Feb	Young Upstart	$ 100.92	12	1,211.04	101.85	1,312.89
Pens	5-Jan-03	4-Feb	Mass Appeal, Inc.	$ 0.12	250	30.75	2.59	33.34
Radio spot	15-Jan-03	14-Feb	WHAT	$ 11.00	15	165.00	13.88	178.88
Billboard	12-Jan-03	11-Feb	Advertising Concepts	$ 101.87	20	2,037.40	171.35	2,208.75
Newspaper	25-Jan-03	24-Feb	Village Reader	$ 65.11	6	390.66	32.85	423.51
Newspaper	1-Feb-03	3-Mar	University Voice	$ 23.91	2	47.82	4.02	51.84
T-Shirts	3-Feb-03	5-Mar	Mass Appeal, Inc.	$ 5.67	200	1,134.00	95.37	1,229.37
Yellow Pages	1-Feb-03	3-Mar	NYNEX	$ 152.94	4	611.76	51.45	663.21
Newspaper	1-Mar-03	31-Mar	University Voice	$ 23.91	2	47.82	4.02	51.84
Blow-in cards	28-Feb-03	30-Mar	Advertising Concepts	$ 0.17	275	47.30	3.98	51.28
Magazine	27-Feb-03	29-Mar	Young Upstart	$ 100.92	12	1,211.04	101.85	1,312.89
Subway	22-Feb-03	24-Mar	Advertising Concepts	$ 35.00	30	1,050.00	88.31	1,138.31
Radio spot	1-Feb-03	3-Mar	WHAT	$ 11.00	30	330.00	27.75	357.75
Newspaper	25-Feb-03	27-Mar	Village Reader	$ 65.11	6	390.66	32.85	423.51
Blow-in cards	10-Mar-03	9-Apr	Advertising Concepts	$ 0.17	275	47.30	3.98	51.28
Radio spot	15-Feb-03	17-Mar	WHAT	$ 11.00	25	275.00	23.13	298.13
Pens	15-Mar-03	14-Apr	Mass Appeal, Inc.	$ 0.12	250	30.75	2.59	33.34
Yellow Pages	1-Mar-03	31-Mar	NYNEX	$ 152.94	4	611.76	51.45	663.21
Subway	20-Mar-03	19-Apr	Advertising Concepts	$ 35.00	30	1,050.00	88.31	1,138.31
Newspaper	1-Apr-03	1-May	University Voice	$ 23.91	2	47.82	4.02	51.84
Subway	10-Apr-03	10-May	Advertising Concepts	$ 35.00	30	1,050.00	88.31	1,138.31
Billboard	28-Mar-03	27-Apr	Advertising Concepts	$ 101.87	20	2,037.40	171.35	2,208.75
name				$ 1,321.89	1784	16,047.15	1,349.57	17,396.72

Practice

► Concepts Review

Label each element of the Excel worksheet window shown in Figure C-23.

FIGURE C-23

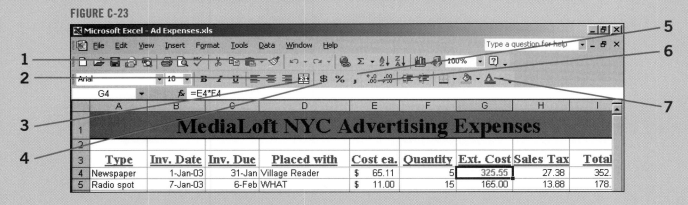

Match each command or button with the statement that describes it.

8. Cells command on the Format menu
9. Delete command on the Edit menu
10. Conditional Formatting
11. [clipboard icon]
12. [$ icon]
13. [spell check icon]

a. Changes appearance of cell depending on result
b. Erases the contents of a cell
c. Used to check the spelling in a worksheet
d. Used to change the appearance of selected cells
e. Pastes the contents of the Clipboard into the current cell
f. Changes the format to Currency

Select the best answer from the list of choices.

14. Which button increases the number of decimal places in selected cells?
   a. [icon]
   b. [icon]
   c. [icon]
   d. [icon]
15. Each of the following operators can be used in conditional formatting, *except*:
   a. Equal to.
   b. Greater than.
   c. Similar to.
   d. Not between.
16. How many conditional formats can be created in any cell?
   a. 1
   b. 2
   c. 3
   d. 4
17. Which button center-aligns the contents of a single cell?
   a. [icon]
   b. [icon]
   c. [icon]
   d. [icon]

18. **Which of the following is an example of the comma format?**
    a. $5,555.55
    b. 5555.55
    c. 55.55%
    d. 5,555.55
19. **What is the name of the feature used to resize a column to its widest entry?**
    a. AutoResize
    b. AutoFormat
    c. AutoFit
    d. AutoAdjust
20. **Which feature applies formatting attributes according to cell contents?**
    a. Conditional Formatting
    b. Comments
    c. AutoFormat
    d. Merge and Center

► Skills Review

1. **Format values.**
   a. Start Excel and open a new workbook.
   b. Enter the information from Table C-6 in your worksheet. Begin in cell A1, and do not leave any blank rows or columns.

TABLE C-6

MediaLoft Great Britain Quarterly Sales Projection			
Department	Average Price	Quantity	Totals
Sports	25	2250	
Computers	40	3175	
History	35	1295	
Personal Growth	25	2065	

   c. Save this workbook as **MediaLoft GB Inventory** in the drive and folder where your Project Files are stored.
   d. Add the bold attribute to the data in the Department column.
   e. Use the Format Painter to paste the format from the data in the Department column to the Department and Totals labels.
   f. Add the italics attribute to the Average Price and Quantity labels.
   g. Apply the Comma format to the Price and Quantity data and reduce the number of decimals in the Quantity column to 0.
   h. Insert formulas in the Totals column (multiply the average price by the Quantity).
   i. Apply the Currency format to the Totals data.
   j. Save your work.
2. **Use fonts and font sizes.**
   a. Select the range of cells containing the column titles.
   b. Change the font of the column titles to Times New Roman.
   c. Increase the font size of the column titles and the title in cell A1 to 14-point.
   d. Resize the columns as necessary.
   e. Select the range of values in the Average Price column.
   f. Format the range using the Currency Style button.
   g. Save your changes.
3. **Change attributes and alignment.**
   a. Select the worksheet title **MediaLoft Great Britain**, then use the Bold button to boldface it.
   b. Use the Merge and Center button to center the title and the Quarterly Sales Projection labels over columns A through D.

c. Select the label **Quarterly Sales Projection**, then apply underlining to the label.

d. Select the range of cells containing the column titles, then center them.

e. Return the underlined, merged and centered Quarterly Sales Projection label to its original alignment.

f. Move the Quarterly Sales Projection label to cell D2 and change the alignment to Align Right.

g. Save your changes, then preview and print the workbook.

4. Adjust column widths.

a Use the Format menu to change the size of the Average Price column to **25**.

b. Use the AutoFit feature to resize the Average Price column.

c. Use the Format menu to resize the Department column to **18** and the Sold column to **11**.

d. Change the text in cell C3 to **Sold**, use AutoFit to resize the column, then change the column size to 11.

e. Save your changes.

5. Insert and delete rows and columns.

a. Insert a new row between rows 4 and 5.

b. Add MediaLoft Great Britain's newest department—**Children's Corner**—in the newly inserted row. Enter **35** for the average price and **1225** for the number sold.

c. Add the following comment to cell A5: **New department**.

d. Add a formula in cell D5 that multiplies the Average Price column by the Sold column.

e. Add a new column between the Department and Average Price columns with the title **Location**.

f. Delete the History row.

g. Edit the comment so it reads "New department. Needs promotion."

h. Save your changes.

6. Apply colors, patterns, and borders.

a. Add an outside border around the Average Price and Sold data.

b. Apply a light green background color to the labels in the Department column.

c. Apply a gold background to the column labels in cells **B3:E3**.

d. Change the color of the font in the column labels in cells B3:E3 to blue.

e. Add a 12.5% Gray pattern fill to the title in Row 1. (*Hint*: Use the Patterns tab in the Format Cells dialog box to locate the 12.5% Gray pattern.)

f. Enter your name in cell A20, then save your work.

g. Preview and print the worksheet, then close the workbook.

7. Use conditional formatting.

a. Open the Project File EX C-2 from the drive and folder where your Project Files are stored, then save it as **Monthly Operating Expenses**.

b. Create conditional formatting that changes the monthly data entry to blue if a value is **greater than 2500**, and changes it to red if **less than 700**.

c. Create a third conditional format that changes the monthly data to green if a value is **between 1000 and 2000**.

d. Use the Bold button and Center button to format the column headings and row titles.

e. Make Column A wide enough to accommodate the contents of cells **A4:A9**.

f. AutoFit the remaining columns.

g. Use Merge and Center in Row 1 to center the title over columns A–E.

h. Format the title in cell A1 using 14-point Times New Roman text. Fill the cell with a color and pattern of your choice.

i. Delete the third conditional format.

j. Enter your name in cell A20, then apply a green background to it and make the text color yellow.

k. Use the Edit menu to clear the cell formats from the cell with your name, then save your changes.

8. Check spelling.

a. Check the spelling in the worksheet using the spell checker, correcting any spelling errors.

b. Save your changes, then preview and print the workbook.

c. Close the workbook, then exit Excel.

▶ Independent Challenge 1

Beautiful You, a small beauty salon, has been using Excel for several months. Now that the salon's accounting records are in Excel, the manager would like you to work on the inventory. Although more items will be added later, the worksheet has enough items for you to begin your modifications.

  a. Start Excel, open the Project File EX C-3 from the drive and folder where your Project Files are stored, then save it as **BY Inventory**.

  b. Create a formula that calculates the value of the inventory on hand for each item.

  c. Use an absolute reference to calculate the sale price of each item, using the markup percentage shown.

  d. Add the bold attribute to the column headings.

  e. Make sure all columns are wide enough to display the data and headings.

  f. Add a row under #2 Curlers for **Nail Files**, price paid **$0.25**, sold **individually (each)**, with **59** on hand.

  g. Verify that all the formulas in the worksheet are correct. Adjust any items as needed, check the spelling, then save your work.

  h. Use conditional formatting to call attention to items with a quantity of 25 or fewer on hand. Use boldfaced red text.

  i. Add an outside border around the data in the Item column.

  j. Delete the row with #3 Curlers.

  k. Enter your name in an empty cell, then save the file.

  l. Preview and print the worksheet, close the workbook, then exit Excel.

▶ Independent Challenge 2

You volunteer several hours each week with the Community Action Center. You would like to examine the membership list, and decide to use formatting to make the existing data look more professional and easier to read.

  a. Start Excel, open the Project File EX C-4 from the drive and folder where your Project Files are stored, then save it as **Community Action**.

  b. Remove any blank columns.

  c. Format the Annual Revenue figures using the Currency format.

  d. Make all columns wide enough to fit their data and headings.

  e. Use formatting enhancements, such as fonts, font sizes, and text attributes to make the worksheet more attractive.

  f. Center-align the column labels.

  g. Use conditional formatting so that Number of Employees data greater than 50 employees appears in a contrasting color.

  h. Before printing, preview the file so you know what the worksheet will look like. Adjust any items as necessary, check spelling, enter your name in an empty cell, save your work, then print a copy.

  i. Close the workbook then exit Excel.

Independent Challenge 3

Classic Instruments is a Miami-based company that manufactures high-quality pens and markers. As the finance manager, one of your responsibilities is to analyze the monthly reports from your five district sales offices. Your boss, Joanne Bennington, has just asked you to prepare a quarterly sales report for an upcoming meeting. Because several top executives will be attending this meeting, Joanne reminds you that the report must look professional. In particular, she asks you to emphasize the company's surge in profits during the last month and to highlight the fact that the Northeastern district continues to outpace the other districts.

a. Plan a worksheet that shows the company's sales during the first quarter. Assume that all pens are the same price. Make sure you include:
- The number of pens sold (units sold) and the associated revenues (total sales) for each of the five district sales offices. The five sales districts include: Northeastern, Midwestern, Southeastern, Southern, and Western
- Calculations that show month-by-month totals and a three-month cumulative total
- Calculations that show each district's share of sales (percent of Total Sales)
- Formatting enhancements to emphasize the recent month's sales surge and the Northeastern district's sales leadership

b. Ask yourself the following questions about the organization and formatting of the worksheet: How will you calculate the totals? What formulas can you copy to save time and keystrokes? Do any of these formulas need to use an absolute reference? How will you show dollar amounts? What information should be shown in bold? Do you need to use more than one font? Should you use more than one point size?

c. Start Excel, then build the worksheet with your own price and sales data. Enter the titles and labels first, then enter the numbers and formulas. You can use the form in Table C-7 to get started.

d. Save the workbook as **Classic Instruments** in the drive and folder where your Project Files are stored.

e. Adjust the column widths as necessary.

f. Change the height of row 1 to 30 points.

g. Format labels and values, and change the attributes and alignment.

h. Use the AutoFormat feature to add color and formatting to the data.

i. Resize columns and adjust the formatting as necessary.

j. Add a column that calculates a 22% increase in sales dollars. Use an absolute cell reference in this calculation.

k. Create a new column named Increased Sales that adds the projected increase to the Total Sales. (*Hint*: Make sure the current formatting is applied to the new information.)

l. Insert a ClipArt image in an appropriate location, adjusting its size and position as necessary.

m. Enter your name in an empty cell.

n. Check the spelling, then save your work.

o. Preview, then print the file in landscape orientation.

p. Close the file then exit Excel.

TABLE C-7

Classic Instruments										
1st Quarter Sales Report										
		January		February		March		Total		
Office	Price	Units Sold	Sales	Units Sold	Sales	Units Sold	Sales	Units Sold	Sales	
Northeastern										
Midwestern										
Southeastern										
Southern										
Western										

Independent Challenge 4

After saving for many years, you now have enough funds to take that international trip you have always dreamed about. Your well-traveled friends have told you that you should always have the local equivalent of $100 U.S. dollars in cash with you when you enter a country. You decide to use the Web to determine how much money you will need in each country.

a. Start Excel, open a new workbook, then save it as **Currency Conversions** in the drive and folder where your Project Files are stored.

b. Enter column and row labels using the following table to get started.

Currency Equivalents			
$100 in US dollars			
Country	$1 Equivalent	$100 US	Name of Units
Australia			
Canada			
France			
Germany			
Sweden			
United Kingdom			

c. Go to the Alta Vista search engine at www.altavista.com and locate information on currency conversions. (*Hint*: One possible site where you can determine currency equivalents is www.oanda.com/. Use the Quick Converter.)

d. Find out how much cash is equivalent to **$1** in U.S. dollars for the following countries: **Australia**, **Canada**, **France**, **Germany**, **Sweden**, and the **United Kingdom**. Also enter the name of the currency used in each country.

e. Create an equation that calculates the equivalent of **$100** in U.S. dollars for each country in the list, using an absolute value in the formula.

f. Format the entries in columns B and C using the correct currency unit for each country, with two decimal places. (*Hint*: Use the Numbers tab in the Format cells dialog box; choose the appropriate currency format from the Symbol list, using 2 decimal places. For example, use the **F (French) Standard** format for the France row, and so forth.)

g. Create a conditional format that changes the font attributes of the calculated amount in the "$100 US" column to bold and red if the amount is equals or exceeds **500 units** of the local currency.

h. Merge and center the title over the column headings.

i. Add a background color to the title.

j. Apply the AutoFormat of your choice to the conversion table.

k. Enter your name in an empty worksheet cell.

l. Spell check, save, preview, then print the worksheet.

m. If you have access to an e-mail account, e-mail your workbook to your instructor as an attachment.

n. Close the workbook and exit Excel.

► Visual Workshop

Create the worksheet shown in Figure C-24, using skills you learned in this unit. Open the Project File EX C-5 from the drive and folder where your Project Files are stored, then save it as **Projected March Advertising Invoices**. Create a conditional format in the Cost ea. column so that entries greater than 60 appear in red. (*Hint*: The only additional font used in this exercise is Times New Roman. It is 22 points in row 1, and 16 points in row 3.) Spell check the worksheet, then save and print your work.

FIGURE C-24

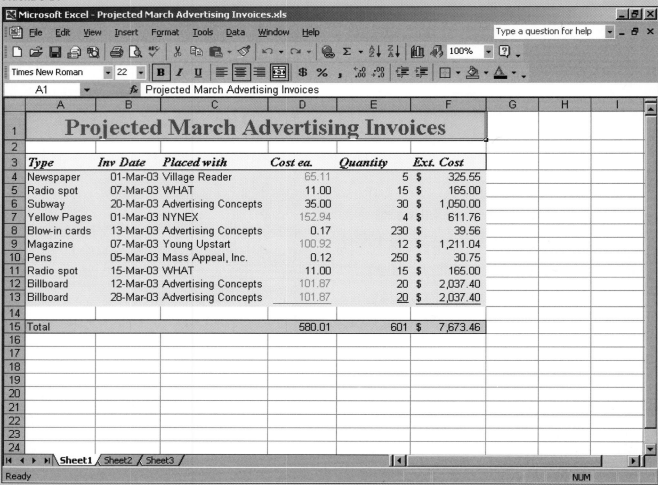

Working
with Charts

► **Plan and design a chart**

[MOUS] ► **Create a chart**

[MOUS] ► **Move and resize a chart**

[MOUS] ► **Edit a chart**

[MOUS] ► **Format a chart**

[MOUS] ► **Enhance a chart**

[MOUS] ► **Annotate and draw on a chart**

[MOUS] ► **Preview and print a chart**

Worksheets provide an effective way to organize information, but they are not always the best format for presenting data to others. Information in a selected range or worksheet can easily be displayed as a chart. Charts, often called graphs, allow you to communicate the relationships in your worksheet data in readily understandable pictures. In this unit, you will learn how to create a chart, how to edit a chart and change the chart type, how to add text annotations and arrows to a chart, and how to preview and print a chart. For the annual meeting Jim Fernandez needs you to create a chart showing the six-month sales history for the MediaLoft stores in the eastern division. He wants to illustrate the growth trend in this division.

Planning and Designing a Chart

Before creating a chart, you need to plan the information you want your chart to show and how you want it to look. In early June, the Marketing Department launched a regional advertising campaign for the eastern division. The results of the campaign were increased sales during the fall months. Jim wants his chart for the annual meeting to illustrate the growth trend for sales in MediaLoft's eastern division stores and to highlight this sales increase.

Details

Jim wants you to use the worksheet shown in Figure D-1 and the following guidelines to plan the chart:

► **Determine the purpose of the chart and identify the data relationships you want to communicate graphically**
You want to create a chart that shows sales throughout MediaLoft's eastern division from July through December. In particular, you want to highlight the increase in sales that occurred as a result of the advertising campaign.

► **Determine the results you want to see, and decide which chart type is most appropriate to use**
Different charts display data in distinctive ways. Some chart types are more appropriate for particular types of data and analyses. How you want your data displayed—and how you want that data interpreted—can help you determine the best chart type to use. Table D-1 describes several different types of charts and indicates when each one is best used. Because you want to compare data (sales in multiple locations) over a time period (the months July through December), you decide to use a column chart.

► **Identify the worksheet data you want the chart to illustrate**
You are using data from the worksheet titled "MediaLoft Eastern Division Stores" shown in Figure D-1. This worksheet contains the sales data for the four stores in the eastern division from July through December.

► **Sketch the chart, then use your sketch to decide where the chart elements should be placed**
You sketch your chart as shown in Figure D-2. You put the months on the horizontal axis (the **x-axis**) and the monthly sales figures on the vertical axis (the **y-axis**). The x-axis is often called the **category axis** because it often contains the names of data groups, such as months or years. The y-axis is called the **value axis** because it often contains numerical values that help you interpret the size of chart elements. (In a 3-D chart, the y-axis is referred to as the z-axis.) The area inside the horizontal and vertical axes is called the **plot area**. The **tick marks** on the y-axis create a scale of measure for each value. Each value in a cell you select for your chart is a **data point**. In any chart, a **data marker** visually represents each data point, which in this case is a column. A collection of related data points is a **data series**. In this chart, there are four data series (Boston, Chicago, Kansas City, and New York), so you include a **legend** to make it easy to identify them.

FIGURE D-1: Worksheet containing sales data

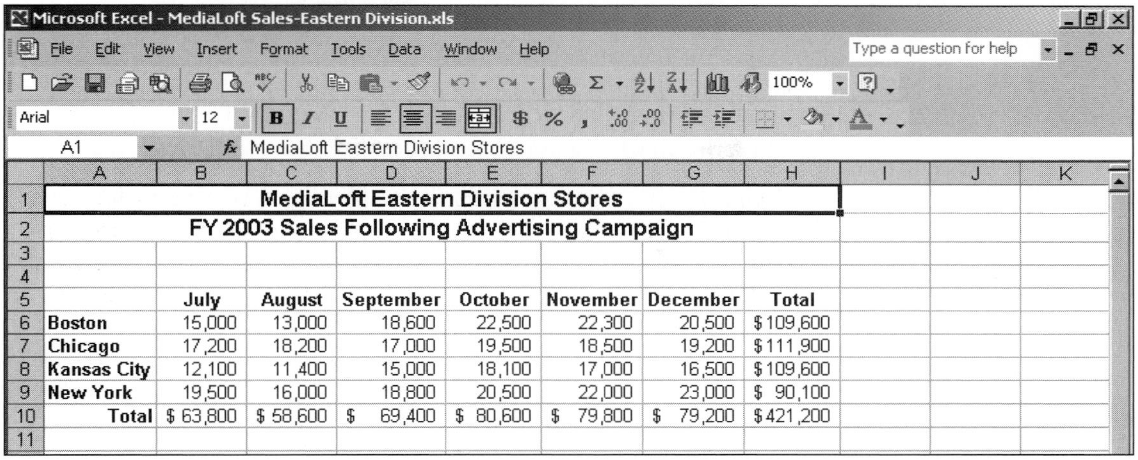

Microsoft Excel - MediaLoft Sales-Eastern Division.xls

File Edit View Insert Format Tools Data Window Help

A1   MediaLoft Eastern Division Stores

	A	B	C	D	E	F	G	H	I	J	K
1	MediaLoft Eastern Division Stores										
2	FY 2003 Sales Following Advertising Campaign										
3											
4											
5		July	August	September	October	November	December	Total			
6	Boston	15,000	13,000	18,600	22,500	22,300	20,500	$109,600			
7	Chicago	17,200	18,200	17,000	19,500	18,500	19,200	$111,900			
8	Kansas City	12,100	11,400	15,000	18,100	17,000	16,500	$109,600			
9	New York	19,500	16,000	18,800	20,500	22,000	23,000	$ 90,100			
10	Total	$ 63,800	$ 58,600	$ 69,400	$ 80,600	$ 79,800	$ 79,200	$421,200			
11											

FIGURE D-2: Column chart sketch

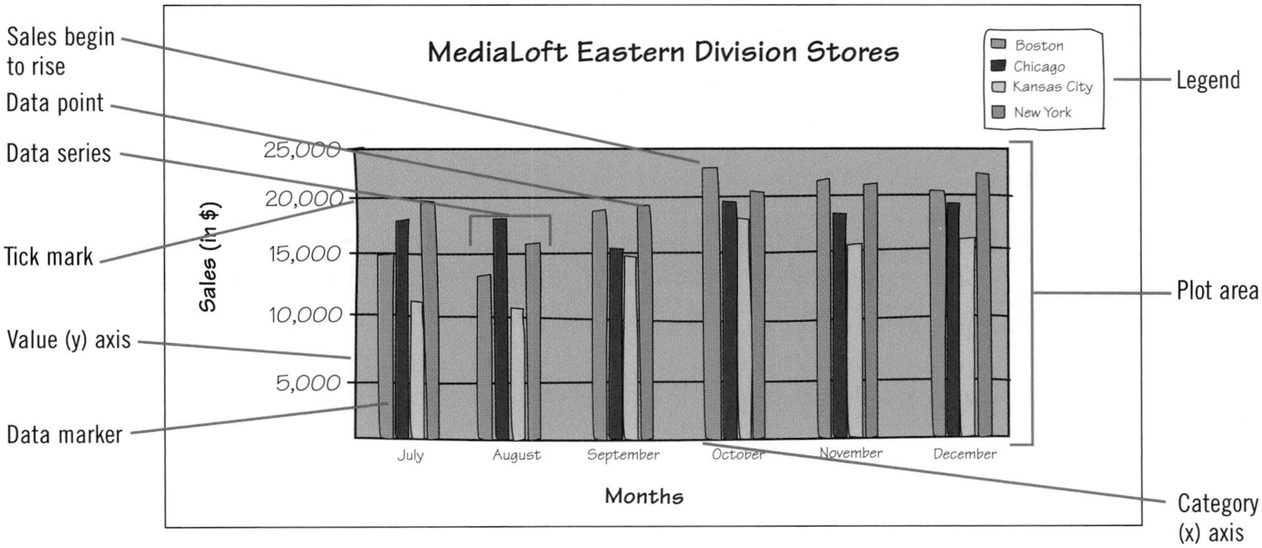

Sales begin to rise
Data point
Data series
Tick mark
Value (y) axis
Data marker

Legend
Plot area
Category (x) axis

TABLE D-1: Commonly used chart types

type	button	description
Area		Shows how individual volume changes over time in relation to total volume
Bar		Compares distinct object levels over time using a horizontal format; sometimes referred to as a horizontal bar chart in other spreadsheet programs
Column		Compares distinct object levels over time using a vertical format; the Excel default; sometimes referred to as a bar chart in other spreadsheet programs
Line		Compares trends over even time intervals; appears similar to an area chart, but does not emphasize total
Pie		Compares sizes of pieces as part of a whole; used for a single series of numbers
XY (scatter)		Compares trends over uneven time or measurement intervals; used in scientific and engineering disciplines for trend spotting and extrapolation
Combination	none	Combines a column and line chart to compare data requiring different scales of measure

Creating a Chart

To create a chart in Excel, you first select the range containing the data you want to chart. Once you've selected a range, you can use the Excel Chart Wizard to lead you through the process of creating the chart. ◄━━━ Using the worksheet containing the sales data for the eastern division, Jim asks you to create a chart that shows the growth trend that occurred as a result of the advertising campaign.

Steps

1. **Start Excel, open the Project File EX D-1 from the drive and location where your Project Files are stored, then save it as MediaLoft Sales - Eastern Division**
   You want the chart to include the monthly sales figures for each of the eastern division stores, as well as month and store labels. You don't include the Total column and row because the monthly figures make up the totals, and these figures would skew the chart.

2. **Select the range A5:G9, then click the Chart Wizard button 📊 on the Standard toolbar**
   The selected range contains the data you want to chart. The Chart Wizard opens. The Chart Wizard - Step 1 of 4 - Chart Type dialog box lets you choose the type of chart you want to create. The default chart type is a Clustered Column, as shown in Figure D-3. You can see a preview of the chart using your selected data by clicking, then holding the **Press and Hold to View Sample** button.

3. **Click Next to accept Clustered Column, the default chart type**
   The Chart Wizard - Step 2 of 4 - Chart Source Data dialog box lets you choose the data to chart and whether the series appear in rows or columns. You want to chart the effect of sales for each store over the time period. Currently, the rows are accurately selected as the data series, as specified by the Series in option button located under the Data range. Because you selected the data before clicking the Chart Wizard button, Excel converted the range to absolute values and the correct range, =Sheet1!$A$5:$G$9, appears in the Data range text box.

4. **Click Next**
   The Chart Wizard - Step 3 of 4 - Chart Options dialog box shows a sample chart using the data you selected. The store locations (the rows in the selected range) are plotted against the months (the columns in the selected range), and Excel added the months as labels for each data series. A legend shows each location and its corresponding color on the chart. The Titles tab lets you add titles to the chart and its axes. Other tabs let you modify the axes, legend, and other chart elements.

5. **Click the Chart title text box, then type MediaLoft Sales - Eastern Division**
   After a moment, the title appears in the Sample Chart box. See Figure D-4.

6. **Click Next**
   In the Chart Wizard - Step 4 of 4 - Chart Location dialog box, you determine the placement of the chart in the workbook. You can display a chart as an object on the current sheet, on any other existing sheet, or on a newly created chart sheet. A **chart sheet** in a workbook contains only a chart, which is linked to the worksheet data. The default selection—displaying the chart as an object in the sheet containing the data—will help Jim emphasize his point at the annual meeting.

7. **Click Finish**
   The column chart appears and the Chart toolbar opens, either docked or floating, as shown in Figure D-5. Your chart might be in a different location and look slightly different. You will adjust the chart's location and size in the next lesson. The **selection handles**, the small squares at the corners and sides of the chart's border, indicate that the chart is selected. Anytime a chart is selected, as it is now, a blue border surrounds the worksheet data range, a green border surrounds the row labels, and a purple border surrounds the column labels.

8. **Click the Save button 💾 on the Standard toolbar**

FIGURE D-3: First Chart Wizard dialog box

Selected chart

Chart types

Clustered column chart is the default

Chart subtypes for selected chart

Description of selected chart subtype

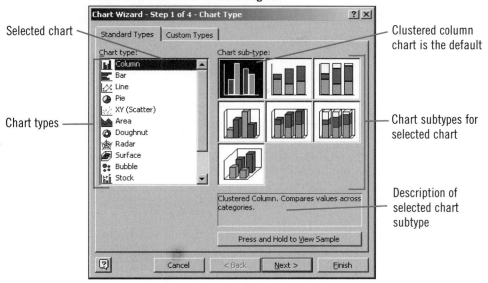

FIGURE D-4: Third Chart Wizard dialog box

Type the chart title here

Sample chart

Title added

Legend

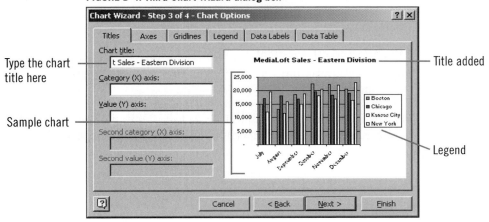

FIGURE D-5: Worksheet with column chart

Column labels

Row labels

Data range

Selected chart object

Chart toolbar title bar

Title

Legend

Selection handles

Month labels on the x-axis

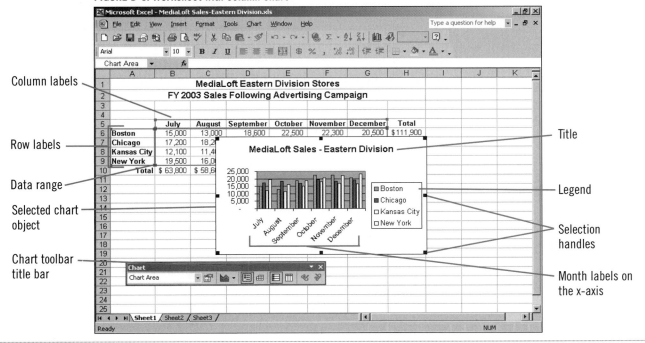

Moving and Resizing a Chart

Charts are graphics, or drawn objects, and are not located in a specific cell or at a specific range address. An **object** is an independent element on a worksheet. You can select an object by clicking within its borders to surround it with selection handles. You can move a selected chart object anywhere on a worksheet without affecting formulas or data in the worksheet. However, any data changed in the worksheet will automatically be updated in the chart. You can resize a chart to improve its appearance by dragging its selection handles. You can even put a chart on another sheet, and it will still reflect the original data. Chart objects contain other objects, such as a title and legend, which you can move and resize. To move an object, select it, then drag it or cut and copy it to a new location. When you select a chart object, the name of the selected object appears in the Chart Objects list box on the Chart toolbar and in the name box. ✍ Jim wants you to increase the size of the chart, position it below the worksheet data, then change the position of the legend.

Steps

1. Make sure the chart is still selected, then position the pointer over the chart

The pointer shape ⌖ indicates that you can move the chart or use a selection handle to resize it. For a table of commonly used chart pointers, refer to Table D-2. On occasion, the Chart toolbar obscures your view. You can dock the toolbar to make it easier to see your work.

2. If the chart toolbar is floating, click the **Chart toolbar's title bar**, drag it to the right edge of the status bar until it docks, then release the mouse button

The toolbar is docked on the bottom of the screen.

3. Place ⌖ on a blank area near the edge of the chart, press and hold the left mouse button, using ✛, drag it until the upper-left edge of the chart is at the top of row 13 and the left edge of the chart is at the left border of column A, then release the mouse button

As you drag the chart, you can see a dotted outline representing the chart's perimeter. The chart appears in the new location.

4. Position the pointer on the right-middle selection handle until it changes to ↔, then drag the right edge of the chart to the right edge of column H

The chart is widened. See Figure D-6.

5. Position the pointer over the top-middle selection handle until it changes to ↕, then drag it to the top of row 12

6. If the labels for the months do not fully appear, position the pointer over the bottom middle selection handle until it changes to ↕, then drag down to display the months

You can move the legend to improve the chart's appearance. You want to align the top of the legend with the top of the plot area.

7. Click the **legend** to select it, then drag the **legend** upward using ⌖ so the top of the legend aligns with the top of the plot area

Selection handles appear around the legend when you click it; "Legend" appears in the Chart Objects list box on the Chart toolbar as well as in the name box, and a dotted outline of the legend perimeter appears as you drag. Changing any label will modify the legend text.

8. Click cell **A9**, type **NYC**, then click ✓

See Figure D-7. The legend changes to the text you entered.

9. Click the **Save button** 🖫 on the Standard toolbar

QuickTip
The Chart menu only appears on the menu bar when a chart or one of its objects is selected.

QuickTip
Resizing a chart doesn't affect the data in the chart, only the way the chart looks on the sheet.

QuickTip
Because the chart is no longer selected, the chart toolbar no longer appears.

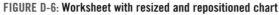

FIGURE D-6: Worksheet with resized and repositioned chart

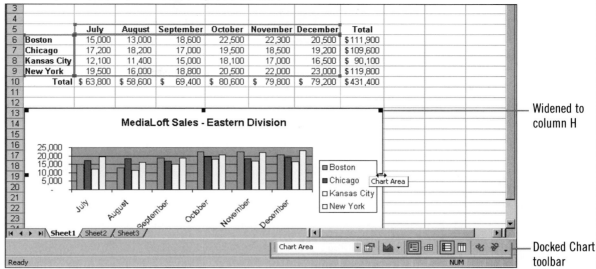

Widened to column H

Docked Chart toolbar

FIGURE D-7: Worksheet with repositioned legend

Repositioned legend

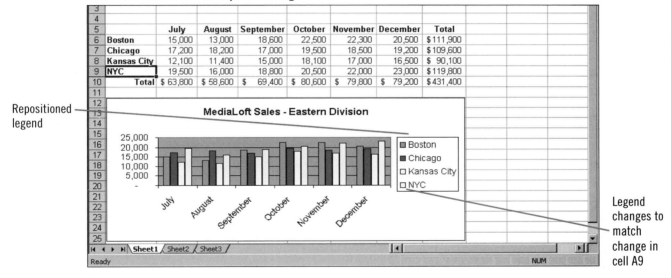

Legend changes to match change in cell A9

TABLE D-2: Commonly used pointers

name	pointer	use	name	pointer	use
Diagonal resizing	↗ or ↖	Change chart shape	**I-beam**	I	Edit chart text from corners
Draw	+	Create shapes	**Move chart**	✛	Change chart location
Horizontal resizing	↔	Change chart shape from left to right	**Vertical resizing**	↕	Changes chart shape from top to bottom

CLUES TO USE

Identifying chart objects

There are many objects within a chart, such as bars and axes; Excel makes it easy to identify each of them. Placing the mouse pointer over a chart object displays a ScreenTip identifying it, whether the chart is selected or not. If a chart—or any object in it—is selected, the ScreenTips still appear. In addition, the name of the selected chart object appears in the Chart Object list box on the Chart toolbar and in the name box.

Editing a Chart

Once you've created a chart, it's easy to modify it. You can change data values in the worksheet, and the chart will automatically be updated to reflect the new data. You can also easily change the type of chart displayed by using the buttons on the Chart toolbar. ✒━━ Jim looks over his worksheet and realizes that he entered the wrong data for the Kansas City store in November and December. After you correct this data, he wants to see how the same data looks using different chart types.

1. If necessary, scroll the worksheet so that you can see both the chart and row 8, containing the Kansas City sales figures, then place your mouse pointer over the December data point to display **Series "Kansas City" Point "December" Value: 16,500**

2. Click cell **F8**, type **19000** to correct the November sales figure, press [➜], type **20500** in cell **G8**, then click ✓

The Kansas City columns for November and December reflect the increased sales figures. See Figure D-8. The totals in column H and row 10 are also updated.

3. Select the chart by clicking on a blank area within the chart border, then click the **Chart Type list arrow** 📊▾ on the Chart toolbar

The chart type buttons appear on the Chart Type palette. Table D-3 describes the principal chart types available.

4. Click the **Bar Chart button** ▤ on the palette

The column chart changes to a bar chart. See Figure D-9. You look at the bar chart, take some notes, then decide to convert it back to a column chart. You now want to see if the large increase in sales would be better presented with a three-dimensional column chart.

5. Click the **Chart Type list arrow** ▤▾, then click the **3-D Column Chart button** 📊 on the palette

A three-dimensional column chart appears. You notice that the three-dimensional column format is more crowded than the two-dimensional format but gives you a sense of volume.

6. Click the **Chart Type list arrow** 📊▾, then click the **Column Chart button** 📊 on the palette

7. Click the **Save button** 💾 on the Standard toolbar

Trouble?
If you cannot see the chart and data together on your monitor, click View on the menu bar, click Zoom, then click 75%.

QuickTip
As you work with charts, experiment with different formats for your charts until you get just the right look.

QuickTip
The chart type button displays the last chart type selected.

TABLE D-3: Commonly used chart type buttons

click to display a	click to display a	click to display a	click to display a
📈 area chart	🥧 pie chart	📊 3-D area chart	🥧 3-D pie chart
▤ bar chart	📉 (XY) scatter chart	📊 3-D bar chart	📄 3-D surface chart
📊 column chart	🍩 doughnut chart	📊 3-D column chart	🗄 3-D cylinder chart
📉 line chart	📡 radar chart	📊 3-D line chart	📊 3-D cone chart

FIGURE D-8: Worksheet with new data entered for Kansas City

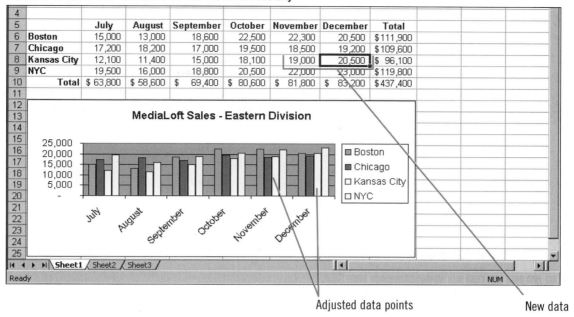

	July	August	September	October	November	December	Total
Boston	15,000	13,000	18,600	22,500	22,300	20,500	$111,900
Chicago	17,200	18,200	17,000	19,500	18,500	19,200	$109,600
Kansas City	12,100	11,400	15,000	18,100	19,000	20,500	$ 96,100
NYC	19,500	16,000	18,800	20,500	22,000	23,000	$119,800
Total	$ 63,800	$ 58,600	$ 69,400	$ 80,600	$ 81,800	$ 83,200	$437,400

Adjusted data points   New data

FIGURE D-9: Bar chart

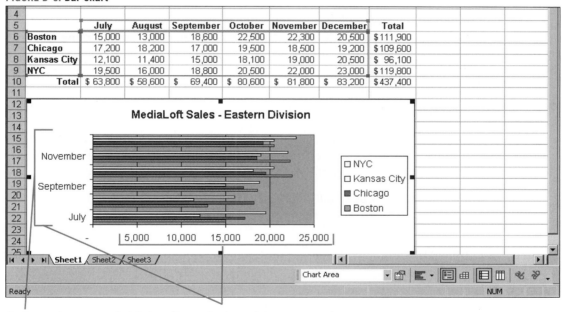

	July	August	September	October	November	December	Total
Boston	15,000	13,000	18,600	22,500	22,300	20,500	$111,900
Chicago	17,200	18,200	17,000	19,500	18,500	19,200	$109,600
Kansas City	12,100	11,400	15,000	18,100	19,000	20,500	$ 96,100
NYC	19,500	16,000	18,800	20,500	22,000	23,000	$119,800
Total	$ 63,800	$ 58,600	$ 69,400	$ 80,600	$ 81,800	$ 83,200	$437,400

Your chart may show more axis labels   Row and column data are reversed

Rotating a 3-D chart

In a three-dimensional chart, other data series in the same chart can sometimes obscure columns or bars. You can rotate the chart to obtain a better view. Click the chart, click the tip of one of its axes (select the Corners object), then drag the handles until a more pleasing view of the data series appears. See Figure D-10.

FIGURE D-10: 3-D chart rotated with improved view of data series

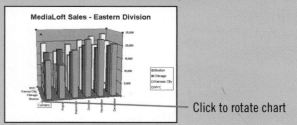

Click to rotate chart

Excel 2002

Formatting a Chart

After you've created a chart using the Chart Wizard, you can easily modify its appearance. You can use the Chart toolbar and Chart menu to change the colors of data series and to add or eliminate a legend and gridlines. **Gridlines** are the horizontal and vertical lines in the chart that enable the eye to follow the value on an axis. The Chart toolbar buttons are listed in Table D-4. ◆ Jim wants you to make some changes in the appearance of his chart. He wants to see if the chart looks better without gridlines, and he wants to change the color of a data series.

Steps 1 2 3 4

1. **Make sure the chart is still selected**
   Horizontal gridlines currently extend from the y-axis tick marks across the chart's plot area.

2. **Click Chart on the menu bar, click Chart Options, click the Gridlines tab in the Chart Options dialog box, then click the Major Gridlines check box for the Value (Y) axis to remove the check**
   The gridlines disappear from the sample chart in the dialog box, as shown in Figure D-11.

3. **Click the Major Gridlines check box for the Value (Y) axis to reselect it, then click the Minor Gridlines check box for the Value (Y) axis**
   Both major and minor gridlines appear in the sample. **Minor gridlines** show the values between the tick marks.

4. **Click the Minor Gridlines check box for the Value (Y) axis, then click OK**
   The minor gridlines disappear, leaving only the major gridlines on the Value axis. You can change the color of the columns to better distinguish the data series.

5. **With the chart selected, double-click any light blue column in the NYC data series**
   Handles appear on all the columns in the NYC data series, and the Format Data Series dialog box opens, as shown in Figure D-12.

QuickTip

Add labels, values, and percentages to your chart by using the Data Labels tab in the Chart Options dialog box.

6. **Click the fuchsia box (fourth row, first column) in the Patterns tab, then click OK**
   All the columns for the series become fuchsia, and the legend changes to match the new color. Compare your finished chart to Figure D-13.

7. **Click the Save button 🔖 on the Standard toolbar**

TABLE D-4: Chart enhancement buttons

button	use
🖼	Displays formatting dialog box for the selected object on the chart
📉	Selects chart type (chart type on button changes to last chart type selected)
📋	Adds/deletes legend
▦	Creates a data table within the chart
📇	Charts data by row
🏛	Charts data by column
✂	Angles selected text downward (clockwise)
🔖	Angles selected text upward (counter clockwise)

FIGURE D-11: Chart Options dialog box

Sample chart
appears without
gridlines

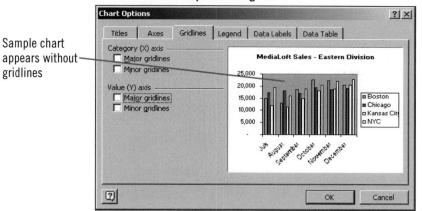

FIGURE D-12: Format Data Series dialog box

Sample of
selected color

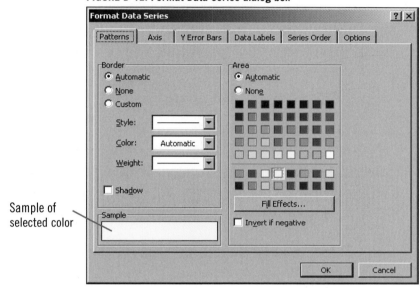

FIGURE D-13: Chart with formatted data series

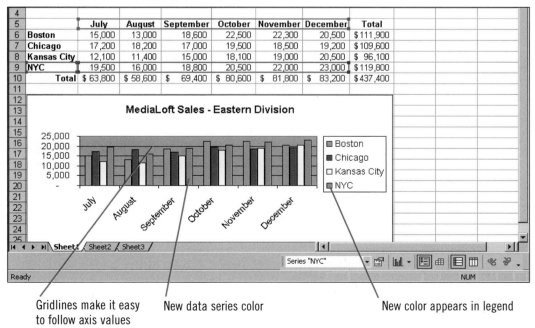

	July	August	September	October	November	December	Total
Boston	15,000	13,000	18,600	22,500	22,300	20,500	$ 111,900
Chicago	17,200	18,200	17,000	19,500	18,500	19,200	$ 109,600
Kansas City	12,100	11,400	15,000	18,100	19,000	20,500	$ 96,100
NYC	19,500	16,000	18,800	20,500	22,000	23,000	$ 119,800
Total	$ 63,800	$ 58,600	$ 69,400	$ 80,600	$ 81,800	$ 83,200	$ 437,400

Gridlines make it easy
to follow axis values

New data series color

New color appears in legend

Enhancing a Chart

There are many ways to enhance a chart to make it easier to read and understand. You can create titles for the x-axis and y-axis, add graphics, or add background color. You can even format the text you use in a chart. ▰▰▰▰▰ Jim wants you to improve the appearance of his chart by creating titles for the x-axis and y-axis and adding a drop shadow to the title.

Steps

1. **Click a blank area of the chart to select it, click Chart on the menu bar, click Chart Options, click the Titles tab in the Chart Options dialog box, then type Months in the Category (X) axis text box**

   Descriptive text on the x-axis helps readers understand the chart. The word "Months" appears below the month labels in the sample chart, as shown in Figure D-14.

   > **QuickTip**
   >
   > To edit the text, position the pointer over the selected text box until it changes to I, click, then edit the text.

2. **In the Value (Y) axis text box, type Sales (in $), then click OK**

   A selected text box containing "Sales (in $)" appears rotated 90 degrees to the left of the y-axis. Once the Chart Options dialog box is closed, you can move the Value or Category axis title to a new position by clicking on an edge of the object then dragging it.

3. **Press [Esc] to deselect the Value-axis title**

   Next you decide that a border with a drop shadow will enhance the chart title.

4. **Click the chart title, MediaLoft Sales – Eastern Division, to select it**

   > **QuickTip**
   >
   > The Format button ▣ opens a dialog box with the appropriate formatting options for the selected chart element. The ScreenTip for the button changes, depending on the selected object.

5. **Click the Format Chart Title button ▣ on the Chart toolbar to open the Format Chart Title dialog box, make sure the Patterns tab is selected, then click the Shadow check box to select it**

   A border with a drop shadow surrounds the title in the Sample area.

6. **Click the Font tab in the Format Chart Title dialog box, click Times New Roman in the Font list, click Bold Italic in the Font style list, click OK, then press [Esc] to deselect the chart title**

   A border with a drop shadow appears around the chart title, and the chart title text is reformatted.

   > **QuickTip**
   >
   > You can also double-click the Category axis title to open the Format Axis Titles dialog box.

7. **Click Months (the Category axis title), click ▣, click the Font tab if necessary, select Times New Roman in the Font list, then click OK**

   The Category axis title appears in the Times New Roman font.

8. **Click Sales (in $) (the Value axis title), click ▣, click the Font tab if necessary, click Times New Roman in the Font list, click OK, then press [Esc] to deselect the title**

   The Value axis title appears in the Times New Roman font. Compare your chart to Figure D-15.

9. **Click the Save button ▣ on the Standard toolbar**

FIGURE D-14: Sample chart with Category (X) axis text

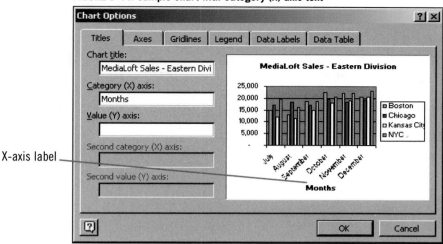

X-axis label

FIGURE D-15: Enhanced chart

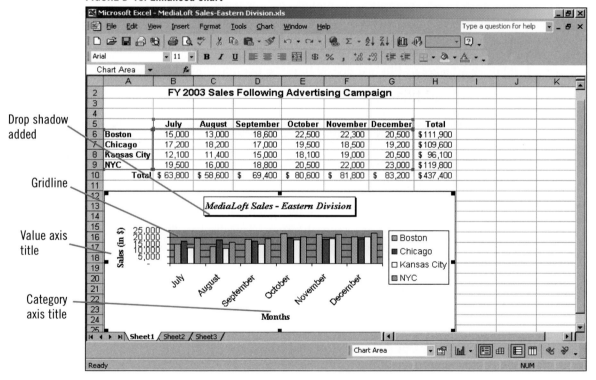

Drop shadow added

Gridline

Value axis title

Category axis title

Clues To Use

Changing text alignment in charts

You can modify the alignment of axis text to make it fit better within the plot area. With a chart selected, double-click the axis text to be modified. The Format Axis dialog box opens. Click the Alignment tab, then change the alignment by typing the number of degrees in the Degrees text box, or by clicking a marker in the Degrees sample box. When you have made the desired changes, click OK.

Annotating and Drawing on a Chart

Excel 2002

You can add arrows and text annotations to point out critical information in your charts. **Text annotations** are labels that you add to a chart to further describe your data. You can draw lines and arrows that point to the exact locations you want to emphasize. Jim wants you to add a text annotation and an arrow to highlight the October sales increase.

Steps

1. **Make sure the chart is selected**

   To call attention to the Boston October sales increase, you can draw an arrow that points to the top of the Boston October data series with the annotation, "Due to ad campaign." With the chart selected, simply typing text in the formula bar creates annotation text.

2. **Type Due to ad campaign, then click the Enter button** ☑

   As you type, the text appears in the formula bar. After you confirm the entry, the text appears in a selected text box within the chart window.

3. **Point to an edge of the text box so that the pointer changes to** 🔖

4. **Drag the text box above the chart, as shown in Figure D-16, then release the mouse button**

   You can add an arrow to point to a specific area or item in a chart by using the Drawing toolbar.

5. **Click the Drawing button** 🖉 **on the Standard toolbar**

   The Drawing toolbar appears below the worksheet.

6. **Click the Arrow button** ↖ **on the Drawing toolbar, then move the pointer over the chart**

   The pointer changes to ╋, and the status bar displays "Click and drag to insert an AutoShape." When you draw an arrow, the point farthest from where you start will have the arrowhead.

7. **Position ╋ under the t in the word "to" in the text box, press and hold the left mouse button, drag the line to the Boston column in the October sales series, then release the mouse button**

   An arrow appears, pointing to Boston October sales. The arrow is a selected object in the chart; you can resize, format, or delete it just like any other object. Compare your finished chart to Figure D-17.

8. **Click** 🖉 **to close the Drawing toolbar**

9. **Click the Save button** 🖫 **on the Standard toolbar**

Trouble?

If the pointer changes to I or ↔, release the mouse button, click outside the text box area to deselect it, select the text box, then repeat Step 3.

QuickTip

To annotate charts, you can also use the Callout shapes on the AutoShapes menu in the Drawing toolbar.

QuickTip

You can also insert text and an arrow in the data section of a worksheet by clicking the Text Box button 📰 on the Drawing toolbar, drawing a text box, typing the text, then adding the arrow.

FIGURE D-16: Repositioning text annotation

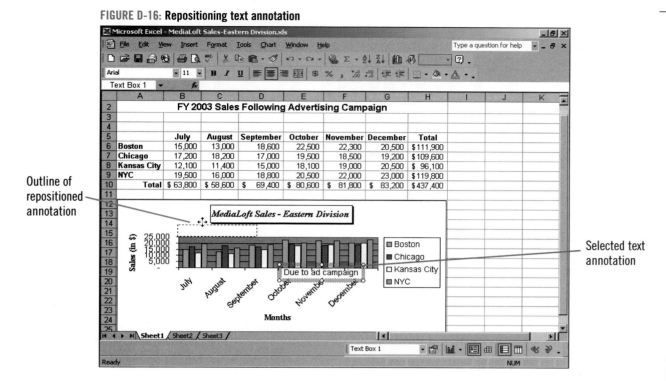

Outline of repositioned annotation

Selected text annotation

FIGURE D-17: Completed chart with text annotation and arrow

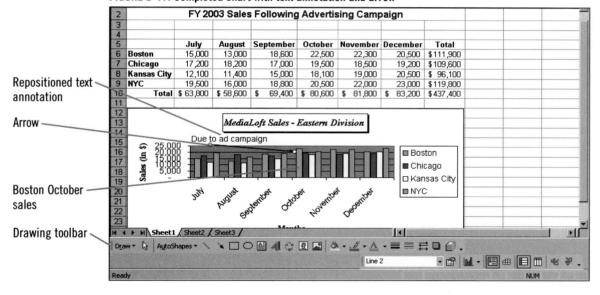

Repositioned text annotation

Arrow

Boston October sales

Drawing toolbar

Exploding a pie slice

Just as an arrow can call attention to a data series, you can emphasize a pie slice by exploding, or pulling it away from, the pie chart. Once the pie chart is selected, click the pie to select it, click the desired slice to select only that slice, then drag the slice away from the pie, as shown in Figure D-18. After you change the chart type, you may need to adjust arrows within the chart.

FIGURE D-18: Exploded pie slice

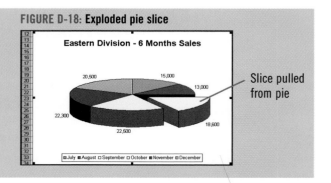

Slice pulled from pie

Previewing and Printing a Chart

After you complete a chart, you will often need to print it. Like previewing a worksheet, previewing a chart lets you see what your chart looks like before you print it. You can print a chart by itself or as part of the worksheet. ⬦━━━ Jim wants a printed version of the chart for the annual meeting. He wants you to print the worksheet and the chart together, so that the shareholders can see the actual sales numbers for the eastern division stores.

Steps

1. Press **[Esc]** to deselect the arrow and the chart, enter your name in cell **A35**, then press **[Ctrl][Home]**

2. Click the **Print Preview button** 🔍 on the Standard toolbar
   The Print Preview window opens. You decide the chart and data would make better use of the page if they were printed in **landscape** orientation—that is, with the text running the long way on the page. You will use Page Setup to change the page orientation.

3. Click **Setup** on the Print Preview toolbar to open the Page Setup dialog box, then click the **Page tab**, if necessary

4. Click the **Landscape option button** in the Orientation section, as shown in Figure D-19, then click **OK**
   Because each page has a default left margin of 0.75", the chart and data will print too far over to the left of the page. You can change this setting using the Margins tab.

5. Click **Setup** on the Print Preview toolbar, click the **Margins tab**, click the **Horizontally check box** (under Center on page), then click **OK**
   The data and chart are positioned horizontally on the page. See Figure D-20.

6. Click **Print** to display the Print dialog box, then click **OK**
   The data and chart print, and you are returned to the worksheet. If you want, you can choose to preview (and print) only the chart.

7. Select the **chart**, then click the **Print Preview button** 🔍
   The chart appears in the Print Preview window. If you wanted to, you could print the chart by clicking the Print button on the Print Preview toolbar.

8. Click **Close** on the Print Preview toolbar

9. Click the **Save button** 💾 on the Standard toolbar, close the workbook, then exit Excel

FIGURE D-19: **Page tab of the Page Setup dialog box**

Landscape option
button selected →

Depending on your
printer, your settings
may differ →

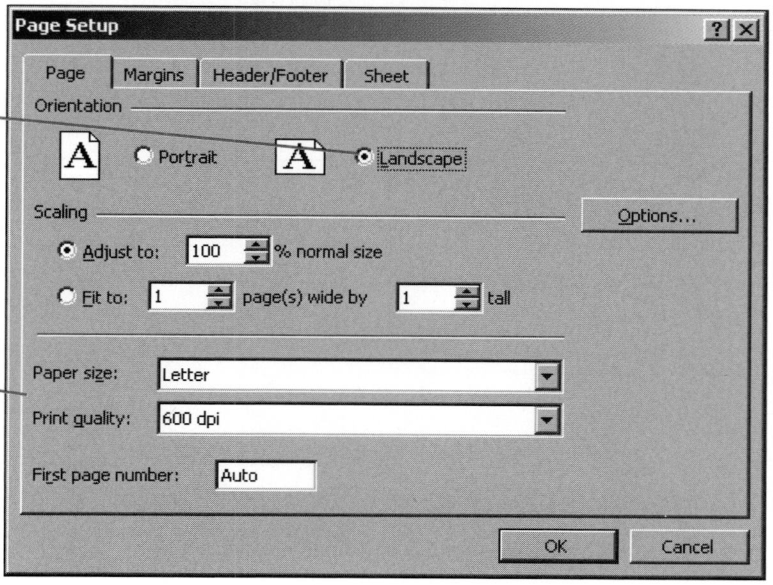

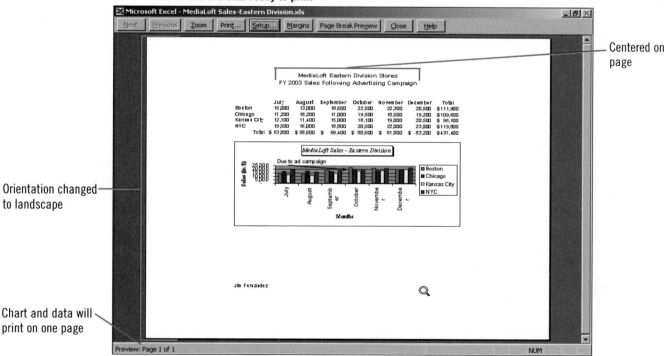

FIGURE D-20: **Chart and data ready to print**

Centered on
page →

Orientation changed
to landscape →

Chart and data will
print on one page →

Using the Page Setup dialog box for a chart

When a chart is selected, a different Page Setup dialog box opens than when neither the chart nor data is selected. The Center on Page options are not always available. To accurately position a chart on the page, you can click the Margins button on the Print Preview toolbar. Margin lines appear on the screen and show you exactly how the margins will appear on the page. The exact placement appears in the status bar when you press and hold the mouse button on the margin line. You can drag the lines to the exact settings you want.

Practice

► Concepts Review

Label each element of the Excel chart shown in Figure D-21.

FIGURE D-21

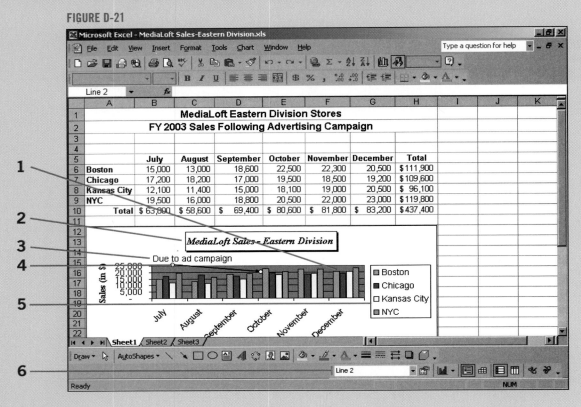

Match each chart type with the statement that describes it.

7. Column
8. Area
9. Pie
10. Combination
11. Line

a. Shows how volume changes over time
b. Compares data as parts of a whole
c. Displays a column and line chart using different scales of measurement
d. Compares trends over even time intervals
e. Compares data over time—the Excel default

Select the best answer from the list of choices.

12. The object in a chart that identifies patterns used for each data series is a:
   a. Data point.
   b. Plot.
   c. Legend.
   d. Range.

13. What is the term for a row or column on a chart?
a. Range address
b. Axis title
c. Chart orientation
d. Data series

14. The orientation of a page whose dimensions are 11" wide by 8½" tall is:
a. Sideways.
b. Longways.
c. Portrait.
d. Landscape.

15. In a 2-D chart, the Value axis is the:
a. X-axis.
b. Z-axis.
c. D-axis.
d. Y-axis.

16. In a 2-D chart, the Category axis is the:
a. X-axis.
b. Z-axis.
c. D-axis.
d. Y-axis.

17. Which pointer is used to resize a chart object?
a.
b.
c.
d.

▶ Skills Review

1. Create a chart.
a. Start Excel, open a new workbook, then save it as **MediaLoft Vancouver Software Usage** in the drive and folder where your Project Files are stored.
b. Enter the information from the following table in your worksheet in range A1:F6. Resize columns as necessary.

	Excel	Word	PowerPoint	Access	Publisher
Accounting	27	15	2	7	1
Marketing	13	35	35	15	35
Engineering	25	5	3	1	5
Personnel	15	25	10	10	27
Production	6	5	22	0	25

   c. Save your work.

   d. Select the range containing the data and headings.

   e. Start the Chart Wizard.

   f. In the Chart Wizard, select a clustered column chart, then verify that the series are in rows; add the chart title **Software Usage by Department**, and make the chart an object on the worksheet.

   g. After the chart appears, save your work.

2. Move and resize a chart.

   a. Make sure the chart is still selected.

   b. Move the chart beneath the data.

   c. Resize the chart so it extends to column L.

   d. Move the legend below the charted data. (*Hint*: Change the legend's position by using the Legend tab in the Chart Options dialog box.)

   e. Save your work.

3. Edit a chart.

   a. Change the value in cell B3 to **6**. Notice the change in the chart.

   b. Select the chart.

   c. Resize the chart so the bottom is at row 24.

   d. Use the Chart Type list arrow to change the chart to a 3-D Column Chart.

   e. Rotate the chart to move the data.

   f. Change the chart back to a column chart.

   g. Save your work.

4. Format a chart.

   a. Make sure the chart is still selected.

   b. Use the Chart Options dialog box to turn off the displayed gridlines.

   c. Change the font used in the Category and Value labels to Times New Roman. (*Hint*: Click the axis to select it, then proceed as you would to change an axis title.)

   d. Turn on the major gridlines for the Value axis.

   e. Change the title's font to Times New Roman.

   f. Save your work.

5. Enhance a chart.

   a. Make sure the chart is selected, then select the **Titles tab** in the Chart Options dialog box.

   b. Enter **Software** as the x-axis title.

   c. Enter **Users** as the y-axis title.

   d. Change **Production** in the legend to **Art**. (*Hint*: Change the text entry in the worksheet.)

   e. Add a drop shadow to the title.

   f. Save your work.

6. Annotate and draw on a chart.
a. Make sure the chart is selected, then create the text annotation **Needs More Users**.
b. Position the text annotation beneath the title.
c. Below the text annotation, use the Drawing toolbar to create an arrow similar to the one in Figure D-22 that points to the area containing the Access data.
d. Save your work.

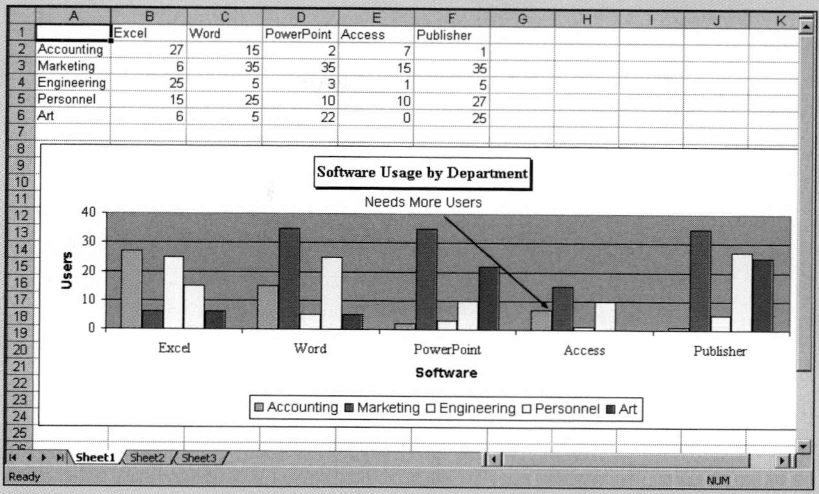

7. Preview and print a chart.
a. In the worksheet, enter your name in cell A30.
b. Preview the chart and data.
c. Change the page orientation to landscape.
d. Center the page contents horizontally and vertically on the page.
e. Print the data and chart from the Print Preview window.
f. Save your work.
g. Preview only the chart, then print it.
h. Close the workbook, then exit Excel.

FIGURE D-22

► Independent Challenge 1

You are the operations manager for the Springfield, Oregon Theater Group. Each year the group applies to various state and federal agencies for matching funds. For this year's funding proposal, you need to create charts to document the number of productions in previous years.

a. Sketch a sample worksheet on a piece of paper describing how you will create the charts. Which type of chart is best suited for the information you need to display? What kind of chart enhancements do you want to use? Will a 3-D effect make your chart easier to understand?
b. Start Excel, open the Project File EX D-2, then save it as **Springfield Theater Group** in the drive and folder where your Project Files are stored.
c. Create a column chart for the data, accepting all Chart Wizard defaults.
d. Change at least one of the colors used in a data series.
e. Create at least two additional charts for the same data to show how different chart types display the same data. (*Hint*: Move each chart to a new location, then deselect each chart before using the Wizard to create the next one.)
f. After creating the charts, make the appropriate enhancements. Include chart titles, legends, and value and category axis titles, using the suggestions in the following table:

suggested chart enhancements	
Title	Types and Number of Plays
Legend	Year 1, Year 2, Year 3, Year 4
Value axis title	Number of Plays
Category axis title	Play Types

Excel 2002

g. Add data labels.

h. Enter your name in a worksheet cell.

i. Save your work. Before printing, preview the file so you know what the charts will look like. Adjust any items as necessary.

j. Print the worksheet (charts and data).

k. Close the workbook, then exit Excel.

▶ Independent Challenge 2

Beautiful You, a small beauty salon, has been using Excel for several months. One of your responsibilities at the Beautiful You Salon is to re-create the company's records using Excel. Another is to convince the current staff that Excel can help them make daily operating decisions more easily and efficiently. To do this, you've decided to create charts using the previous year's operating expenses, including rent, utilities, and payroll. The manager will use these charts at the next monthly meeting.

a. Decide which data in the worksheet should be charted. Sketch two sample charts. What type of charts are best suited for the information you need to show? What kind of chart enhancements will be necessary?

b. Start Excel, open the Project File EX D-3 from the drive and folder where your Project Files are stored, then save it as **BY Expense Charts**.

c. Create a column chart on the worksheet, containing the expense data for all four quarters.

d. Using the same data, create an area chart and one additional chart using any other appropriate chart type. (*Hint*: move each chart to a new location, then deselect it before using the Wizard to create the next one.)

e. Add annotated text and arrows to the column chart that highlight any important data or trends.

f. In one chart, change the color of a data series, then in another chart, use black-and-white patterns only. (*Hint*: use the Fill Effects button in the Format Data Series dialog box. Then display the Patterns tab. Adjust the Foreground color to black and the Background color to white, then select a pattern.

g. Enter your name in a worksheet cell.

h. Save your work. Before printing, preview each chart so you know what the charts will look like. Adjust any items as needed.

i. Print the charts.

j. Close the workbook, then exit Excel.

▶ Independent Challenge 3

You are working as an account representative at the Bright Light Ad Agency. You have been examining the expenses charged to clients of the firm. The Board of Directors wants to examine certain advertising expenses and has asked you to prepare charts that can be used in this evaluation.

a. Start Excel, open the Project File EX D-4 from the drive and folder where your Project Files are stored, then save it as **Bright Light**.

b. Decide what types of charts would be best suited for the data in the range A16:B24. Sketch two sample charts. What kind of chart enhancements will be necessary?

c. Use the Chart Wizard to create at least three different types of charts that show the distribution of advertising expenses. (*Hint*: Move each chart to a new location, then deselect it before using the Wizard to create the next one.)

d. Add annotated text and arrows highlighting important data, such as the largest expense.

e. Change the color of at least one data series.

f. Add chart titles and Category and Value axis titles. Format the titles with a font of your choice. Place a drop shadow around the chart title.

g. Enter your name in a worksheet cell.

h. Save your work. Before printing, preview the file so you know what the charts will look like. Adjust any items as needed. Be sure the chart is placed appropriately on the page.

i. Print the charts, close the workbook then exit Excel.

Independent Challenge 4

Your company, Film Distribution, is headquartered in Montreal, and is considering opening a new office in the U.S. They would like you to begin investigating possible locations. You can use the Web to find and compare median pay scales in specific cities to see how relocating will affect the standard of living for those employees who move to the new office.

a. Start Excel, open a new workbook, then save it as **New Location Analysis** in the drive and folder where your Project Files are located.

b. Connect to the Internet, use your browser to go to homeadvisor.msn.com/pickaplace/comparecities.asp. (If this address is no longer current, go to homeadvisor.msn.com or www.homefair.com, and follow links for **Moving and Relocation**, **Compare Cost of Living**, or similar links to find the information needed for your spreadsheet. You can also use your favorite search engine to locate other sites on cost of living comparisons.)

c. Determine the median incomes for Seattle, San Francisco, Dallas, Salt Lake City, Memphis, and Boston. Record this data on a sheet named Median Income in your workbook. (*Hint*: See the table below for suggested data layout.)

Location	Income
Seattle	
San Francisco	
Dallas	
Salt Lake City	
Memphis	
Boston	

d. Format the data so it looks attractive and professional.

e. Create any type of column chart, with the data series in columns, on the same worksheet as the data. Include a descriptive title.

f. Determine how much an employee would need to earn in Seattle, San Francisco, Dallas, Memphis, and Boston to maintain the same standard of living as if the company chose to relocate to Salt Lake City and pay $75,000. Record this data on a sheet named **Standard of Living** in your workbook.

g. Format the data so it looks attractive and professional.

h. Create any type of chart you feel is appropriate on the same worksheet as the data. Include a descriptive title.

i. Do not display the legends in either chart.

j. Change the color of the data series in the Standard of Living chart to bright green.

k. Remove the major gridlines in the Median Income chart.

l. Format the Value axis in both charts so that the salary income displays a 1000 separator (comma) but no decimal places.

m. Enter your name in a cell in both worksheets.

n. Save the workbook. Preview the chart and change margins as necessary.

o. Print each worksheet, including the data and chart, making setup modifications as necessary.

p. Close the workbook, then exit Excel.

▶ Visual Workshop

Modify a worksheet, using the skills you learned in this unit and using Figure D-23 for reference. Open the Project File EX D-5 from the drive and folder where your Project Files are stored, then save it as **Quarterly Advertising Budget**. Create the chart, then change the chart to reflect Figure D-23. Enter your name in cell A13, save, preview, then print your results.

FIGURE D-23

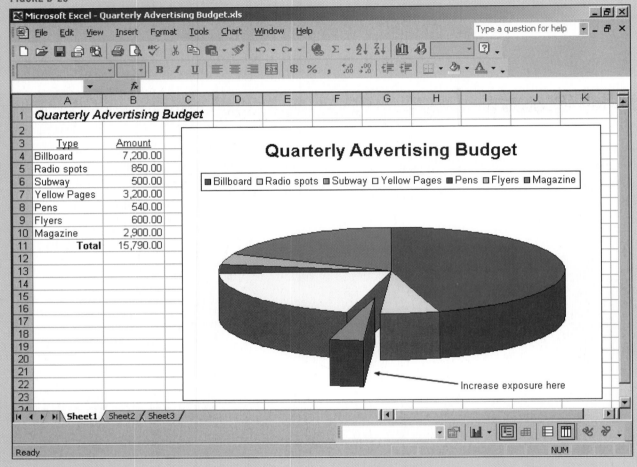

Unit **E**

Working
with Formulas and Functions

Objectives

- ☐MOUS ► **Create a formula with several operators**
- ☐MOUS ► **Use names in a formula**
- ► **Generate multiple totals with AutoSum**
- ☐MOUS ► **Use dates in calculations**
- ☐MOUS ► **Build a conditional formula with the IF function**
- ☐MOUS ► **Use statistical functions**
- ☐MOUS ► **Calculate payments with the PMT function**
- ☐MOUS ► **Display and print formula contents**

Without formulas, Excel would simply be an electronic grid with text and numbers. Used with formulas, Excel becomes a powerful data analysis software tool. As you learn how to analyze data using different types of formulas, including those that call for functions, you will discover more ways to use Excel. In this unit, you will gain a further understanding of Excel formulas and learn how to build several Excel functions. Top management at MediaLoft has asked Jim Fernandez to analyze various company data. To do this, Jim creates several worksheets that require the use of formulas and functions. Because management is considering raising salaries for store managers, Jim has asked you to create a report that compares the payroll deductions and net pay for store managers before and after a proposed raise.

Excel 2002

Creating a Formula with Several Operators

You can create formulas that contain a combination of cell references (for example, Z100 and B2), operators (for example, * [multiplication] and - [subtraction]), and values (for example, 99 or 1.56). Formulas can also contain functions. You have used AutoSum to insert the Sum function into a cell. You can also create a single formula that performs several calculations. If you enter a formula with more than one operator, Excel performs the calculations in a particular sequence based on algebraic rules, called the order of precedence (also called the order of operations); that is, Excel performs the operation(s) within the parentheses first, then performs the other calculations in a specific order. See Table E-1. Jim has been given the gross pay and payroll deductions for the monthly payroll and needs to complete his analysis. He has also preformatted, with the Comma style, any cells that are to contain values. He asks you to enter a formula for net pay that subtracts the payroll deductions from gross pay.

Steps

1. **Start Excel if necessary, open the Project File EX E-1 from the drive and folder where your Project Files are stored, then save it as Company Data**
   The first part of the net pay formula will go in cell B11.

2. **Click Edit on the menu bar, click Go To, type B11 in the Reference box, then click OK**
   Cell B11 is now the active cell. The Go To command is especially useful when you want to select a cell in a large worksheet.

> **Trouble?**
> If you make a mistake while building a formula, press [Esc] and begin again.

3. **Type =, click cell B6, type -, then click the Insert Function button 𝑓x on the formula bar to open the Insert Function dialog box**
   You type the equal sign (=) to tell Excel that a formula follows. B6 references the cell containing the gross pay, and the minus sign (-) indicates that the next entry, a sum, will be subtracted from cell B6. The Function Wizard begins by displaying the Insert Function dialog box, which allows you to choose from a list of available functions or search for a specific function. See Figure E-1.

4. **Type Sum in the Search for a function text box, click Go, make sure Sum is selected in the Select a function list, then click OK**
   B6:B10 appears in the Number1 text box. You want to sum the range B7:B10.

5. **With the Number1 argument selected in the Function Arguments dialog box, click the Number1 Collapse Dialog box button 🔳, select the range B7:B10 in the worksheet, click the Redisplay Dialog Box button 🔳, then click OK**
   Collapsing the dialog box allows you to select the worksheet range. The net pay for Payroll Period 1 appears in cell B11.

6. **Copy the formula in cell B11 into cells C11:F11, then return to cell A1**
   The formula in cell B11 is copied to the range C11:F11 to complete row 11. See Figure E-2.

7. **Save the workbook**

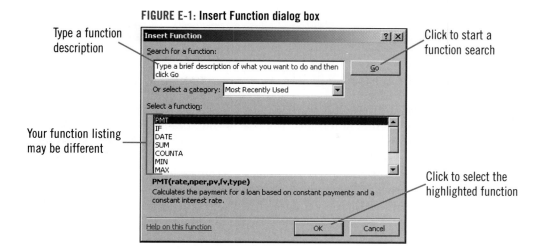

FIGURE E-1: Insert Function dialog box

Type a function description

Click to start a function search

Your function listing may be different

Click to select the highlighted function

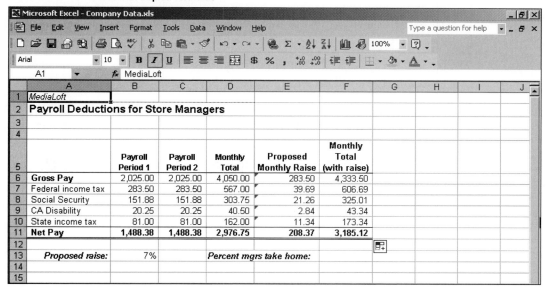

FIGURE E-2: Worksheet with copied formulas

TABLE E-1: Sample formulas using parentheses and several operators

formula	order of precedence	calculated result
=10-20/10-5	Divide 20 by 10; subtract the result from 10, then subtarct 5	3
=(10-20)/10-5	Subtract 20 from 10; divide that by 10; then subtract 5	-6
=(10*2)*(10+2)	Multiply 10 by 2; add 10 to 2; then multiply the results	240

CLUES TO USE

Using Paste Special to paste formulas and values and to perform calculations

You can use the Paste Special command to quickly enter formulas and values or even to perform quick calculations. Click the cell(s) containing the formula or value you want to copy, click the Copy button 📋 on the Standard toolbar, then right-click the cell where you want the result to appear. In the pop-up menu, choose Paste Special, choose the feature you want to paste, then click OK.

Using Names in a Formula

To reduce errors and make your worksheet easier to follow, you can assign names to cells and ranges. You can also use names in formulas to make formulas easier to build. For example, the formula Revenue-Cost is much easier to understand than the formula A2-D3. When used in formulas, names become absolute cell references by default. Names can use uppercase or lowercase letters as well as digits. After you name a cell or range, you can use the name on any sheet in the workbook. If you move a named cell or range, its name moves with it. ◀▬▬▬ Jim wants to include a formula that calculates the percentage of monthly gross pay the managers would actually take home (their net pay) if they received a 7% raise. He asks you to name the cells you'll use in the calculation.

Steps

QuickTip

You can also assign names to ranges of cells. Select the range, click the name box, then type in the range name. You can also name a range by pointing to Name on the Insert menu then choosing Define to provide the name.

QuickTip

You can use the Label Ranges dialog box (Insert menu, Name submenu, Label command) to designate existing column or row headings as labels. Then instead of using cell references for the column or row in formulas, you can use the labels. (If this feature is not turned on, go to Tools/Options/Calculation tab/Accept labels in formulas.)

QuickTip

To delete a cell or range name, click Insert on the menu bar, point to Name, then click Define. Select the name, click Delete, then click OK.

1. **Click cell F6, click the name box on the formula bar to select the active cell reference, type Gross_with_Raise, then press [Enter]**
   The name assigned to cell F6, Gross_with_Raise, appears in the name box. Note that you must type underscores instead of spaces between words. Cell F6 is now named Gross_with_Raise to refer to the monthly gross pay amount that includes the 7% raise. The name box displays as much of the name as fits (Gross_with_...). The net pay cell needs a name.

2. **Click cell F11, click the name box, type Net_with_Raise, then press [Enter]**
   The new formula will use names instead of cell references.

3. **Click cell F13, type =Net_with_Raise/Gross_with_Raise, then click the Enter button ☑ on the formula bar (make sure you begin the formula with an equal sign)**
   Notice that as you finish typing each name, the name changes color to match the outline around the cell reference. The formula bar now shows the new formula, and the result, 0.735, appears in the cell. You can also insert names in a formula by clicking Insert on the menu bar, pointing to Name, then clicking Paste. If you want to replace existing formula references with the corresponding names you have added, click Insert on the menu bar, point to Name, click Apply, click the name or names, then click OK. Cell F13 needs to be formatted in Percent style.

4. **Select cell F13 if necessary, click Format on the menu bar, click Style, click the Style name list arrow, click Percent, then click OK**
   The result shown in cell F13, 74%, is rounded to the nearest whole percent, as shown in Figure E-3. A **style** is a combination of formatting characteristics, such as bold, italic, and underlined. You can use the Style dialog box instead of the Formatting toolbar to apply styles. You can also use it to remove styles: select the cell that has a style and select Normal in the Style name list. To define your own style (such as bold, italic, and 14 point), select a cell, format it using the Formatting toolbar, open the Style dialog box and type a name for your style, then click Add. Later, you can apply all those formatting characteristics by applying your new style from the dialog box.

5. **Add your name to cell A20, save the workbook, then preview and print the worksheet**

FIGURE E-3: Worksheet formula that includes cell names

Name box

Formula with cell names

	A	B	C	D	E	F	G	H	I	J
1	*MediaLoft*									
2	**Payroll Deductions for Store Managers**									
3										
4										
5		**Payroll Period 1**	**Payroll Period 2**	**Monthly Total**	**Proposed Monthly Raise**	**Monthly Total (with raise)**				
6	**Gross Pay**	2,025.00	2,025.00	4,050.00	283.50	4,333.50				
7	Federal income tax	283.50	283.50	567.00	39.69	606.69				
8	Social Security	151.88	151.88	303.75	21.26	325.01				
9	CA Disability	20.25	20.25	40.50	2.84	43.34				
10	State income tax	81.00	81.00	162.00	11.34	173.34				
11	**Net Pay**	**1,488.38**	**1,488.38**	**2,976.75**	**208.37**	**3,185.12**				
12										
13	***Proposed raise:***	7%		***Percent mgrs take home:***		74%				
14										

Cell named Gross_with_Raise

Result of calculation

Cell named Net_with_Raise

F13 = Net_with_Raise/Gross_with_Raise

CLUES TO USE

Producing a list of names

You might want to verify the names you have in a workbook and the cells they reference. To paste a list of names in a workbook, select a blank cell that has several blank cells beside and beneath it. Click Insert on the menu bar, point to Name, then click Paste. In the Paste Name dialog box, click Paste List. Excel produces a list of names that includes the sheet name and the cell or range the name identifies. See Figure E-4.

FIGURE E-4: Worksheet with pasted list of names

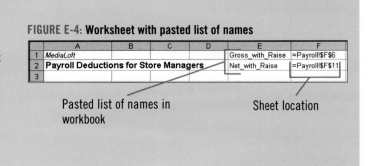

	A	B	C	D	E	F
1	*MediaLoft*				Gross_with_Raise	=Payroll!$F$6
2	**Payroll Deductions for Store Managers**				Net_with_Raise	=Payroll!$F$11
3						

Pasted list of names in workbook

Sheet location

Excel 2002

Generating Multiple Totals with AutoSum

In most cases, the result of a function is a value derived from a single calculation. You have used AutoSum to produce a total of a single range of numbers; you can also use it to total multiple ranges. If you include blank cells to the right or at the bottom of a selected range, AutoSum will generate several totals and enter the results in the blank cells. You can have Excel generate grand totals of worksheet subtotals by selecting a range of cells and using the AutoSum function. ✎ Maria Abbott, MediaLoft's general sales manager, has given Jim a worksheet summarizing store sales. He asks you to complete the worksheet totals.

Trouble?

If you select the wrong combination of cells, click on a single cell and begin again.

1. Make the Sales sheet active, select range **B5:E9**, press and hold **[Ctrl]**, then select range **B11:E15**

To select nonadjacent cells, you must press and hold [Ctrl] while selecting the additional cells. Compare your selections with Figure E-6. The totals will appear in the last line of each selection.

2. Click the **AutoSum button** Σ on the Standard toolbar

When the selected range you want to sum (B5:E9 and B11:E15, in this example) includes a blank cell with data values above it, AutoSum enters the total in the blank cell.

3. Select the range **B5:F17**, then click Σ

Whenever the selected range you want to sum includes a blank cell in the bottom row or right column, AutoSum enters the total in the blank cell. In this case, Excel ignores the data values and totals only the sums. Although Excel generates totals when you click the AutoSum button, it is a good idea to check the results.

4. Click cell **B17**

The formula bar reads =SUM(B15,B9). See Figure E-7. When generating grand totals, Excel references the cells contained in SUM functions with a comma separator between cell references. Excel uses commas to separate multiple arguments in all functions, not just in SUM.

5. Enter your name into cell A20, save the workbook, then preview and print the worksheet

Quick calculations with AutoCalculate

To view a total quickly without entering a formula, just select the range you want to sum, and the answer appears in the status bar next to SUM=. You also can perform other quick calculations, such as averaging or finding the minimum value in a selection. To do this, right-click the AutoCalculate area in the status bar and select from the list of options. The option you select remains in effect and in the status bar until you make another selection. See Figure E-5.

FIGURE E-5: Using AutoCalculate

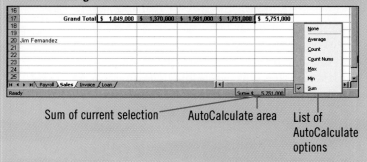

Sum of current selection   AutoCalculate area   List of AutoCalculate options

FIGURE E-6: Selecting nonadjacent ranges using [Ctrl]

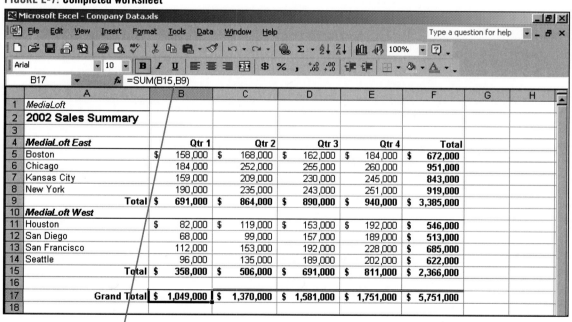

	A	B	C	D	E
1	*MediaLoft*				
2	**2002 Sales Summary**				
3					
4	*MediaLoft East*	Qtr 1	Qtr 2	Qtr 3	Qtr 4
5	Boston	$ 158,000	$ 168,000	$ 162,000	$ 184,000
6	Chicago	184,000	252,000	255,000	260,000
7	Kansas City	159,000	209,000	230,000	245,000
8	New York	190,000	235,000	243,000	251,000
9	Total				
10	*MediaLoft West*				
11	Houston	$ 82,000	$ 119,000	$ 153,000	$ 192,000
12	San Diego	68,000	99,000	157,000	189,000
13	San Francisco	112,000	153,000	192,000	228,000
14	Seattle	96,000	135,000	189,000	202,000
15	Total				
16					
17	Grand Total				
18					

Cell reference box: B11 fx 82000

FIGURE E-7: Completed worksheet

Cell reference box: B17 fx =SUM(B15,B9)

	A	B	C	D	E	F	G	H
1	*MediaLoft*							
2	**2002 Sales Summary**							
3								
4	*MediaLoft East*	Qtr 1	Qtr 2	Qtr 3	Qtr 4	Total		
5	Boston	$ 158,000	$ 168,000	$ 162,000	$ 184,000	$ 672,000		
6	Chicago	184,000	252,000	255,000	260,000	951,000		
7	Kansas City	159,000	209,000	230,000	245,000	843,000		
8	New York	190,000	235,000	243,000	251,000	919,000		
9	Total	$ 691,000	$ 864,000	$ 890,000	$ 940,000	$ 3,385,000		
10	*MediaLoft West*							
11	Houston	$ 82,000	$ 119,000	$ 153,000	$ 192,000	$ 546,000		
12	San Diego	68,000	99,000	157,000	189,000	$ 513,000		
13	San Francisco	112,000	153,000	192,000	228,000	$ 685,000		
14	Seattle	96,000	135,000	189,000	202,000	$ 622,000		
15	Total	$ 358,000	$ 506,000	$ 691,000	$ 811,000	$ 2,366,000		
16								
17	Grand Total	$ 1,049,000	$ 1,370,000	$ 1,581,000	$ 1,751,000	$ 5,751,000		
18								

Comma separates multiple arguments

Excel 2002

Using Dates in Calculations

If you enter dates in a worksheet in a format that Excel recognizes as a date, you can sort them and perform date calculations. When you enter an Excel date format, Excel converts it to a serial number so it can be used in calculations. A date's serial number is the number of days it is from January 1, 1900. Excel assigns the serial number of "1" to January 1, 1900 and counts up from there; the serial number of January 1, 2003, for example, is 37,622. Jim's next task is to calculate the due date and age of each invoice on the worksheet. He reminds you to enter the worksheet dates in a format that Excel recognizes, so he can use date calculations.

Steps

1. Make the Invoice sheet active, click cell **C4**, click the **Insert Function button** on the formula bar, type **Date** in the Search for a function text box, click **Go**, click **Date** in the Select a function list, then click **OK**

   The calculations will be based on a current date of 4/1/03, the date that Jim is revising his worksheet.

2. Enter **2003** in the Year text box, enter **4** in the month text box, enter **1** in the Day text box, then click **OK**

   The date appears in cell C4 as 4/1/03. The Date function uses the format DATE(year, month, day). You want to enter a formula that calculates the invoice due date, which is 30 days from the invoice date. The formula adds 30 days to the invoice date.

   ### Trouble?

   If the year appears with four digits instead of two, your system administrator may have set a four-digit year display. You can continue with the lesson.

3. Click cell **E7**, type =, click cell **B7**, type **+30**, then click the **Enter button** on the formula bar

   Excel calculates the result by converting the 3/1/03 invoice date to a serial date number, adding 30 to it, then automatically formatting the result as the date 3/31/03, as shown in Figure E-8. You can use the same formula to calculate the due dates of the other invoices.

4. Drag the fill handle to copy the formula in cell E7 into cells **E8:E13**

   Relative cell referencing adjusts the copied formula to contain the appropriate cell references. Now you are ready to enter the formula that calculates the age of each invoice. You do this by subtracting the invoice date from the current date. Because each invoice age formula must refer to the current date, you must make cell C4, the current date cell, an absolute reference in the formula.

   ### QuickTip

   You can also perform time calculations in Excel. For example, you can enter an employee's starting and ending time, then calculate how long he or she worked. You must enter time in an Excel time format.

5. Click cell **F7**, type =, click cell **C4**, press **[F4]** to add the absolute reference symbols ($), type -, click **B7**, then click

   The formula bar displays the formula $C$4-B7. The numerical result, 31, appears in cell F7 because there are 31 days between 3/1/03 and 4/1/03. You can use the same formula to calculate the age of the remaining invoices.

   ### QuickTip

   You can also insert the current date into a worksheet by using the TODAY() function. The NOW() function inserts the current date and time into a cell.

6. Drag the fill handle to copy the formula in F7 to the range **F8:F13**, then return to cell A1

   The age of each invoice appears in column F, as shown in Figure E-9.

7. Save the workbook

FIGURE E-8: Worksheet with formula for invoice due date

Formula is invoice date +30

Formula result automatically calculated as date

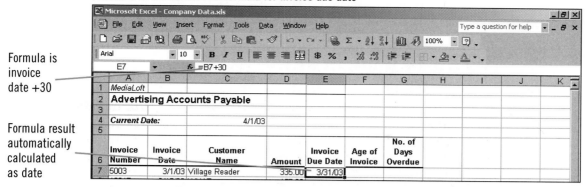

FIGURE E-9: Worksheet with copied formulas

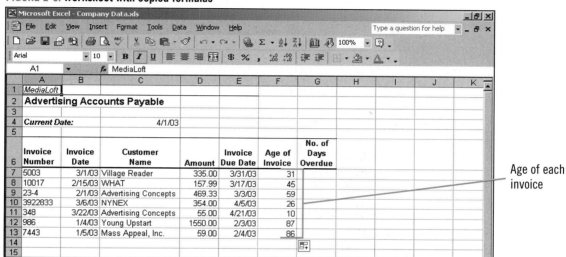

Age of each invoice

Custom number and date formats

When you use numbers and dates in worksheets or calculations, you can use built-in Excel formats or create your own. For example, 9/1/03 uses the Excel format m/d/yy, but you could change it to the format d-mmm, or 1-Sep. The value $3,789 uses the number format $#,### where # represents positive numbers. To apply number formats, click Format on the menu bar, click Cells, then click the Number tab. In the category list, click a category, then specify the exact format in the list or scroll box to the right. To create a custom format, click Custom in the category list, then click a format that resembles the one you want. In the Type box, edit the symbols until they represent the format you want, then click OK. See Figure E-10.

FIGURE E-10: Custom formats on the Number tab in the Format Cells dialog box

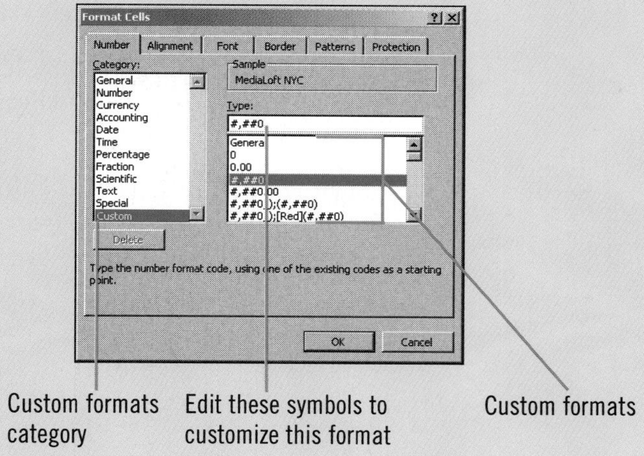

Custom formats category

Edit these symbols to customize this format

Custom formats

Excel 2002

Building a Conditional Formula with the IF Function

You can build a conditional formula using an IF function. A **conditional formula** is one that makes calculations based on stated conditions. For example, you can build a formula to calculate bonuses based on a person's performance rating. If a person is rated a 5 (the stated condition) on a scale of 1 to 5, with 5 being the highest rating, he or she receives 10% of his or her salary as a bonus; otherwise, there is no bonus. A condition that can be answered with a true or false response is called a **logical test**. The IF function has three parts, separated by commas: a condition or logical test, an action to take if the logical test or condition is true, then an action to take if the logical test or condition is false. Another way of expressing this is: IF(test_cond,do_this,else_this). Translated into an Excel IF function, the formula to calculate bonuses would look something like this: IF(Rating=5,Salary*0.10,0). The translation would be: If the rating equals 5, multiply the salary by 0.10 (the decimal equivalent of 10%), then place the result in the selected cell; if the rating does not equal 5, place a 0 in the cell. When entering the logical test portion of an IF statement, you typically use some combination of the comparison operators listed in Table E-2. ✐⎯ You are almost finished with the invoice worksheet. To complete it, you need to use an IF function that calculates the number of days each invoice is overdue.

1. Click cell **G7**, click the **Insert Function button** 🔣 on the formula bar, enter **Conditional** in the Search for a function text box, click **Go**, click **IF** in the Select a function list, then click **OK**

   You want the function to calculate the number of days overdue as follows: If the age of the invoice is greater than 30, calculate the days overdue (Age of Invoice - 30), and place the result in cell G7; otherwise, place a 0 (zero) in the cell.

2. Enter **F7>30** in the Logical_test text box

   The symbol (>) represents "greater than". So far, the formula reads: If Age of Invoice is greater than 30 (in other words, if the invoice is overdue). The next part of the function tells Excel the action to take if the invoice is over 30 days old.

3. Enter **F7-30** in the Value_if_true text box

   This part of the formula is what you want Excel to do if the logical test is true (that is, if the age of the invoice is over 30). Continuing the translation of the formula, this part means: Take the Age of Invoice value and subtract 30. The last part of the formula tells Excel the action to take if the logical test is false (that is, if the age of the invoice is 30 days or less).

4. Enter **0** in the Value_if_false text box, then click **OK**

   The function is complete, and the result, 1 (the number of days overdue), appears in cell G7. See Figure E-11.

5. Copy the formula in cell G7 into cells **G8:G13** and return to cell A1

   Compare your results with Figure E-12.

6. Save the workbook

FIGURE E-11: Worksheet with IF function

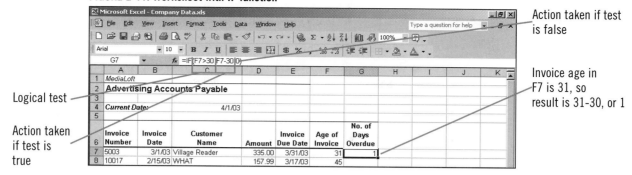

Action taken if test is false

Logical test

Action taken if test is true

Invoice age in F7 is 31, so result is 31-30, or 1

FIGURE E-12: Completed worksheet

	A	B	C	D	E	F	G	H	I	J	K
1	MediaLoft										
2	Advertising Accounts Payable										
3											
4	Current Date:			4/1/03							
5											
6	Invoice Number	Invoice Date	Customer Name	Amount	Invoice Due Date	Age of Invoice	No. of Days Overdue				
7	5003	3/1/03	Village Reader	335.00	3/31/03	31	1				
8	10017	2/15/03	WHAT	157.99	3/17/03	45	15				
9	23-4	2/1/03	Advertising Concepts	469.33	3/3/03	59	29				
10	3922833	3/6/03	NYNEX	354.00	4/5/03	26	0				
11	348	3/22/03	Advertising Concepts	55.00	4/21/03	10	0				
12	986	1/4/03	Young Upstart	1550.00	2/3/03	87	57				
13	7443	1/5/03	Mass Appeal, Inc.	59.00	2/4/03	86	56				
14											
15											

TABLE E-2: Comparison operators

operator	function	operator	function
<	Less than	<=	Less than or equal to
>	Greater than	>=	Greater than or equal to
=	Equal to	<>	Not equal to

CLUES TO USE

Correcting circular references

A cell with a circular reference contains a formula that refers to its own cell location. If you accidentally enter a formula with a circular reference, a warning box will open alerting you to the problem. Click OK to display the Circular Reference toolbar or HELP to open a Help window explaining how to find the circular reference. In simple formulas, a circular reference is easy to spot. To correct it, edit the formula to remove any reference to the cell where the formula is located.

Using Statistical Functions

Excel offers several hundred worksheet functions. A small group of these functions calculates statistics such as averages, minimum values, and maximum values. See Table E-3 for a brief description of these commonly used functions. Now that you have experience using the Function Wizard, you'll type in a few of the more common functions. ✎ Jim wants to present summary information about open accounts payable. To do this, he asks you to add some statistical functions to the worksheet. You begin by using the MAX function to calculate the maximum value in a range.

Steps 1234

1. **Click cell D19, type =MAX(, select range G7:G13, then press [Enter]**
   Excel automatically adds the closing parenthesis. The age of the oldest invoice (or maximum value in range G7:G13) is 57 days, as shown in cell D19. Jim needs to know the largest dollar amount among the outstanding invoices.

2. **In cell D20, type =MAX(, select range D7:D13, then press [Enter]**
   The largest outstanding invoice, of 1550.00, is shown in cell D20. The MIN function finds the smallest dollar amount and the age of the newest invoice.

> **Trouble?**
> If your results do not match those shown here, check your formulas and make sure you did not type a comma following each open parenthesis. The formula in cell D20, for example, should be =MAX(D7:D13).

3. **In cell D21, type =MIN(, select range D7:D13, then press [Enter]; in cell D22, type =MIN(, select range F7:F13, then press [Enter]**
   The smallest dollar amount owed is 55.00, as shown in cell D21, and the newest invoice is 10 days old. The COUNT function calculates the number of invoices by counting the number of entries in column A.

4. **In cell D23, click the Insert Function button [fx] on the formula bar to open the Insert Function dialog box**

> **QuickTip**
> If you don't see the desired function in the Function name list, scroll to display more function names.

5. **Click the Select a category list arrow, choose Statistical, then in the Select a function box, click COUNT**
   After selecting the function name, notice that the description of the COUNT function reads, "Counts the number of cells that contain numbers…" Because the invoice numbers are formatted in General rather than in the Number format, they are considered text entries, not numerical entries, so the COUNT function will not work. There is another function, COUNTA, that counts the number of cells that are not empty and therefore can be used to count the number of invoice number entries.

6. **Under Select a function, click COUNTA, then click OK**
   The Function Arguments dialog box opens and automatically references the range above the active cell as the first argument (in this case, range D19:D22, which is not the range you want to count). See Figure E-13. You need to select the correct range of invoice numbers.

> **QuickTip**
> Instead of using the Collaspe dialog box button, you can click the desired worksheet cell to insert a cell address.

7. **With the Value1 argument selected in the Function Arguments dialog box, click the Value1 Collapse Dialog Box button [▦], select range A7:A13 in the worksheet, click the Redisplay Dialog Box button [▦], click OK, then return to cell A1**
   Cell D23 confirms that there are seven invoices. Compare your worksheet with Figure E-14.

8. **Enter your name in cell A26, save the workbook, then print the worksheet**

FIGURE E-13: Formula Palette showing COUNTA function

Click to pick a
different function

Default range
is incorrect

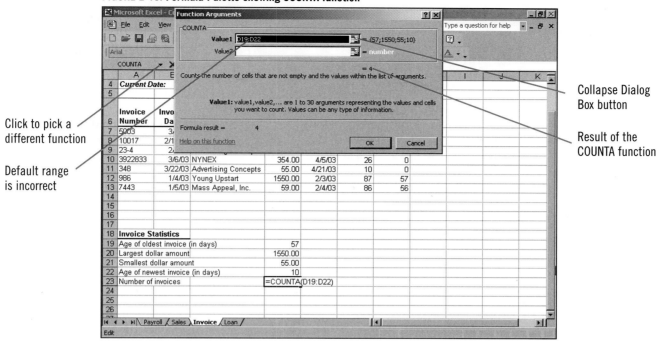

Collapse Dialog
Box button

Result of the
COUNTA function

FIGURE E-14: Worksheet with invoice statistics

Number of
invoices in
A7:A13

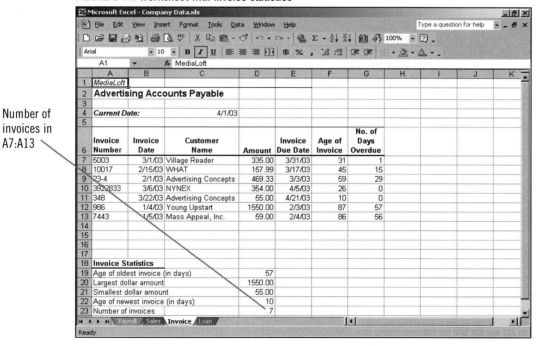

TABLE E-3: Commonly used statistical functions

function	worksheet action	function	worksheet action
AVERAGE	Calculates an average value	MAX	Finds the largest value
COUNT	Counts the number of values	MIN	Finds the smallest value
COUNTA	Counts the number of nonblank entries	MEDIAN	Finds the middle value

Calculating Payments with the PMT Function

PMT is a financial function that calculates the periodic payment amount for money borrowed. For example, if you want to borrow money to buy a car, the PMT function can calculate your monthly payment on the loan. Let's say you want to borrow $15,000 at 8.5% interest and pay the loan off in five years. The Excel PMT function can tell you that your monthly payment will be $311.38. The parts of the PMT function are: PMT(rate, nper, pv, fv, type). See Figure E-15 for an illustration of a PMT function that calculates the monthly payment in the car loan example. ✎ For several months, MediaLoft management has been discussing the expansion of the San Diego store. Jim has obtained quotes from three different lenders on borrowing $27,000 to begin the expansion. He obtained loan quotes from a commercial bank, a venture capitalist, and an investment banker. He wants you to summarize the information, using the Excel PMT function.

Steps 1234

1. Make the Loan sheet active, click cell **E5**, click the **Insert Function button** 𝑓ₓ on the formula bar, enter **PMT** in the Search for a function text box, click **Go**, click **PMT** in the Select a function list if necessary, then click **OK**

2. Move the Function Arguments dialog box to display row 5 of the worksheet; with the cursor in the Rate text box, click cell **C5** on the worksheet, type **/12**, then press **[Tab]**

3. With the cursor in the Nper text box, click cell **D5**; click the PV text box, click cell **B5**, then click **OK**

   You must divide the annual interest by 12 because you are calculating monthly, not annual, payments. The FV and Type are optional arguments. Note that the payment of ($587.05) in cell E5 appears in red, indicating that it is a negative amount. Excel displays the result of a PMT function as a negative value to reflect the negative cash flow the loan represents to the borrower. To show the monthly payment as a positive number, you place a minus sign in front of the PV cell reference in the function.

4. Edit cell E5 so it reads **=PMT(C5/12,D5,-B5)**, then click ☑

   A positive value of $587.05 now appears in cell E5. See Figure E-16. You can use the same formula to generate the monthly payments for the other loans.

5. With cell **E5** selected, drag the fill handle to fill the range **E6:E7**

   A monthly payment of $883.95 for the venture capitalist loan appears in cell E6. A monthly payment of $1,270.98 for the investment banker loan appears in cell E7. The loans with shorter terms have much higher payments. You will not know the entire financial picture until you calculate the total payments and total interest for each lender.

6. Click cell **F5**, type **=E5*D5**, then press **[Tab]**; in cell G5, type **=F5-B5**, then click ☑

7. Copy the formulas in cells F5:G5 into the range **F6:G7**, then return to cell **A1**

   You can experiment with different interest rates, loan amounts, or terms for any one of the lenders; the PMT function generates a new set of values automatically. Compare your results with those in Figure E-17.

8. Enter your name in cell A13, save the workbook, then preview and print the worksheet

FIGURE E-15: Example of PMT function for car loan

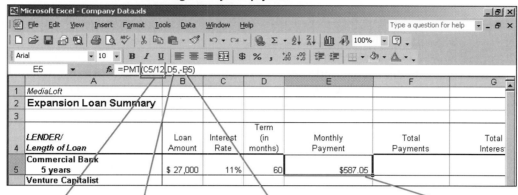

$$PMT(.085/12, 60, 15000) = \$311.38$$

Interest rate per period (rate) — Number of payments (nper) — Present value of loan amount (pv) — Monthly payment calculated

FIGURE E-16: PMT function calculating monthly loan payment

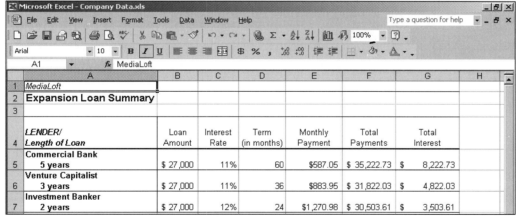

Annual interest rate ÷ 12 months — Loan term — Loan amount (preceded by a minus sign) — Monthly payment calculated

FIGURE E-17: Completed worksheet

Calculating future value with the FV function

You can use the FV (Future Value) function to determine the amount of money a given monthly investment will amount to, at a given interest rate after a given number of payment periods. The syntax is similar to that of the PMT function: FV(rate,nper,pmt,pv,type). For example, suppose you want to invest $1,000 every month for the next 12 months into an account that pays 12% a year, and you want to know how much you will have at the end of 12 months (that is, its future value). You would enter the function FV(.01,12,-1000), and Excel would return the value $12,682.50 as the future value of your investment. As with the PMT function, the units for the rate and nper must be consistent. If you made monthly payments on a three-year loan at 6% annual interest, you would use the rate .06/12 and 36 periods (12*3). The arguments pv and type are optional; pv is the present value, or the total amount the series of payments is worth now. If you omit it, Excel assumes the pv is 0. The "type" argument indicates when the payments are made; 0 is the end of the period, and 1 is the beginning of the period.

Excel 2002

Displaying and Printing Formula Contents

Excel usually displays the result of formula calculations in the worksheet area and displays formula contents for the active cell in the formula bar. However, you can instruct Excel to display the formulas directly in the worksheet cells in which they were entered. You can document worksheet formulas by first displaying the formulas, then printing them. These formula printouts are valuable paper-based worksheet documentation. Because formulas are often longer than their corresponding values, landscape orientation is the best choice for printing formulas. ✐ Jim wants you to produce a formula printout to submit with the worksheet.

1. **Click Tools on the menu bar, click Options, then click the View tab**
   The View tab of the Options dialog box appears, as shown in Figure E-18.

2. **Under Window options, click the Formulas check box to select it, then click OK**
   The columns widen and retain their original formats.

   QuickTip

   Move the Formula Auditing toolbar if necessary.

   ---

3. **Scroll horizontally to bring columns E through G into view**
   Instead of displaying formula results in the cells, Excel shows the actual formulas and automatically adjusts the column widths to accommodate them.

4. **Click the Print Preview button 🔍 on the Standard toolbar**
   The status bar reads Preview: Page 1 of 2, indicating that the worksheet will print on two pages. You want to print it on one page and include the row number and column letter headings.

   QuickTip

   All Page Setup options—such as Landscape orientation, Fit to scaling—apply to the active worksheet and are saved with the workbook.

   ---

5. **Click Setup in the Print Preview window, then click the Page tab**

6. **Under Orientation, click the Landscape option button; then under Scaling, click the Fit to option button and note that the wide and tall check boxes contain the number "1".**
   Selecting Landscape instructs Excel to print the worksheet sideways on the page. The Fit to option ensures that the document is printed on a single page.

   QuickTip

   To print row and column labels on every page of a multiple-page worksheet, click the Sheet tab, and fill in the Rows to repeat at top and the Columns to repeat at left in the Print titles section.

   ---

7. **Click the Sheet tab, under Print click the Row and column headings check box to select it, click OK, then position the Zoom pointer 🔍 over column A and click**
   The worksheet formulas now appear on a single page, in landscape orientation, with row (number) and column (letter) headings. See Figure E-19.

8. **Click Print in the Print Preview window, then click OK**
   After you retrieve the printout, you want to return the worksheet to displaying formula results. You can do this easily by using a key combination.

9. **Press [Ctrl][`] to redisplay formula results**
   [Ctrl][`] (grave accent mark) toggles between displaying formula results and displaying formula contents.

10. **Save the workbook, then close it and exit Excel**
    The completed figure for the payroll worksheet is displayed in Figure E-3; the completed sales worksheet is displayed in Figure E-7; and the completed invoice worksheet is shown in Figure E-14.

FIGURE E-18: View tab of the Options dialog box

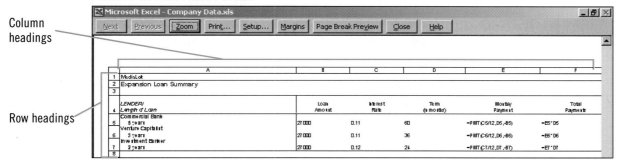

Select this
option to view
formulas

FIGURE E-19: Print Preview window

Column
headings

Row headings

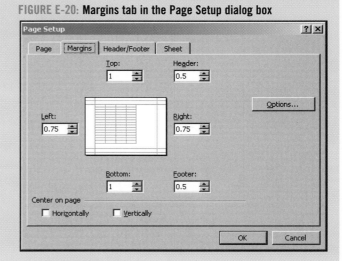

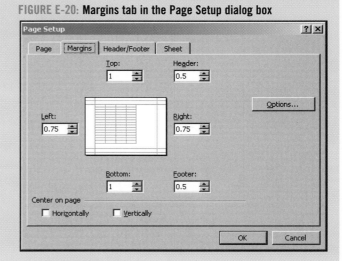

Setting margins and alignment when printing part of a worksheet

You can set custom margins to print smaller sections of a worksheet. Select the range you want to print, click File on the menu bar, click Print, under Print what click Selection, then click Preview. In the Print Preview window, click Setup, then click the Margins tab. See Figure E-20. Double-click the margin numbers and type new ones. Use the Center on page check boxes to center the range horizontally or vertically. If you plan to print the range again, save the view after you print: Click View on the menu bar, click Custom Views, click Add, then type a view name and click OK.

FIGURE E-20: Margins tab in the Page Setup dialog box

Practice

► Concepts Review

Label each element of the Excel screen shown in Figure E-21.

FIGURE E-21

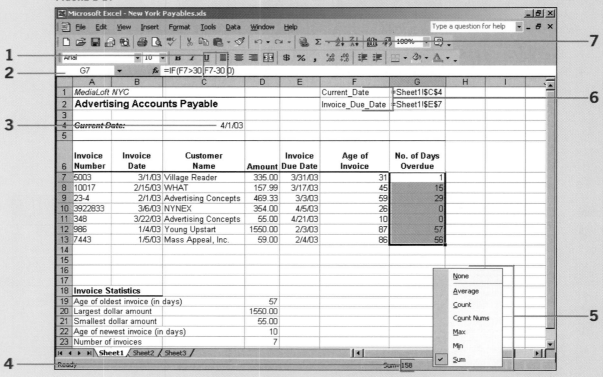

Match each term with the statement that best describes its function.

8. Style
9. COUNTA
10. test_cond
11. COUNT
12. pv

a. Part of the IF function in which the conditions are stated
b. Function used to count the number of numerical entries
c. Part of the PMT function that represents the loan amount
d. Function used to count the number of nonblank entries
e. A combination of formatting characteristics

Select the best answer from the list of choices.

13. To generate a positive payment value when using the PMT function, you must:
- **a.** Enter the function arguments as positive values.
- **b.** Enter the function arguments as negative values.
- **c.** Enter the amount being borrowed as a negative value.
- **d.** Enter the interest rate divisor as a negative value.

14. When you enter the rate and nper arguments in a PMT function, you must:
- **a.** Multiply both units by 12.
- **b.** Be consistent in the units used.
- **c.** Divide both values by 12.
- **d.** Use monthly units instead of annual units.

15. To express conditions such as less than or equal to, you can use a(n):
- **a.** IF function.
- **b.** Comparison operator.
- **c.** AutoCalculate formula.
- **d.** PMT function.

16. Which of the following statements is false?
- **a.** $#,### is an Excel number format.
- **b.** You can create custom number and date formats in Excel.
- **c.** You can use only existing number and date formats in Excel.
- **d.** m/d/yy is an Excel date format.

▶ Skills Review

1. Create a formula with several operators.
- **a.** Start Excel, open the Project File EX E-2 from the drive and folder where your Project Files are stored, then save the workbook as **Manager Bonuses**.
- **b.** On the Bonuses worksheet, select cell **C15** using the Go To command.
- **c.** Enter the formula **C13+(C14*7)**.
- **d.** Use the Paste Special command to paste the values and formats in B4:B10 to G4:G10, then save your work.

2. Use names in a formula.
- **a.** Name cell C13 **Dept_Bonus**.
- **b.** Name cell C14 **Project_Bonus**.
- **c.** Select the range **C4:C10** and name it **Base_Pay**.
- **d.** In cell E4, enter the formula **Dept_Bonus*D4+Project_Bonus**.
- **e.** Copy the formula in cell E4 into the range E5:E10.
- **f.** Format range E4:E10 with the Comma style, using the Style dialog box.
- **g.** Select the range **E4:E10** and name it **Bonus_Total**.
- **h.** In cell F4, enter a formula that sums Base_Pay and Bonus_Total.
- **i.** Copy the formula in cell F4 into the range F5:F10.
- **j.** Format range F4:F10 with the Comma style, using the Style dialog box.
- **k.** Save your work.

3. Generate multiple totals with AutoSum.
a. Select range **E4:F11**.

b. Enter the totals using AutoSum.

c. Format range E11:F11 with the Currency style, using the Style dialog box.

d. Enter your name in cell A18, save your work, then preview and print this worksheet.

4. Use dates in calculations.
a. Make the Merit Pay sheet active.

b. In cell D6, enter the formula **B6+183**.

c. Copy the formula in cell D6 into the range D7:D14.

d. Use the NOW function to insert the date and time in cell A3, widening the column as necessary.

e. In cell E18, enter the text **Next Pay Date**, and, in cell G18, use the Date function to enter the date **10/1/03**. (*Hint*: You must enter the year as 2003. You can format it as a two-digit year using the Modify button on the Style dialog box and choosing Date in the Category list on the Number tab.)

f. Save your work.

5. Build a conditional formula with the IF function.
a. In cell F6, use the Function Wizard to enter the formula **IF(C6=5,E6*0.05,0)**.

b. Copy the formula in cell F6 into the range F7:F14.

c. Apply the comma format with no decimal places to F6:F14.

d. Select the range **A4:G4** and delete the cells, using the Delete command on the Edit menu. Shift the remaining cells up.

e. Repeat the procedure to delete the cells A15:G15.

f. Use the Cells command on the Insert menu to insert a cell between Department Statistics and Average Salary, moving the remaining cells down.

g. Check your formulas to make sure the cell references have been updated.

h. Save your work.

6. Use statistical functions.
a. In cell C18, enter a function to calculate the average salary in the range E5:E13 with no decimal places. Use dragging to select the cells.

b. In cell C19, enter a function to calculate the largest bonus in the range F5:F13.

c. In cell C20, enter a function to calculate the lowest performance rating in the range C5:C13.

d. In cell C21, enter a function to calculate the number of entries in range A5:A13.

e. Enter your name into cell A28, then save, preview, and print the worksheet.

7. Calculate payments with the PMT function.
a. Make the Loan sheet active.

b. In cell B9, use the Function Wizard to enter the formula **PMT(B5/12,B6,-B4)**.

c. In cell B10, enter the formula **B9*B6**.

d. AutoFit column B, if necessary.

e. In cell B11, enter the formula **B10-B4**.

f. Enter your name in cell A15, then save, preview, and print the worksheet.

8. **Display and print formula contents.**
   a. Use the View tab in the Options dialog box to display formulas.
   b. Adjust the column widths as necessary.
   c. Save, preview, and print this worksheet in landscape orientation with the row and column headings.
   d. Redisplay the formula results in the worksheet.
   e. Close the workbook, then exit Excel.

▶ Independent Challenge 1

As manager of Mike's Ice Cream Parlor, you have been asked to create a worksheet that totals the monthly sales of all store products. Your monthly report should include the following:

- Sales totals for the current month for each product
- Sales totals for the last month for each product
- The percent change in sales from last month to this month

To document the report further, you decide to include a printout of the worksheet formulas.

a. Start Excel, open the Project File EX E-3 from the drive and folder where your Project Files are stored, then save it as **Mike's Sales**.
b. Use the TODAY function to enter today's date in cell A3. Create and apply a custom format for the date entry.
c. Complete the headings for weeks 2 through 4. Enter totals for each week, and current month totals for each product. Calculate the percent change in sales from last month to this month. (*Hint*: The formula in words would be (Current Month-Last Month)/Last Month.)
d. After you enter the percent change formula for regular ice cream, copy the formula down the column and format the column with the Percent style.
e. Apply a comma format with no decimal places to all numbers and totals.
f. Enter your name into cell A15, then save, preview, and print the worksheet on a single page. If necessary, print in landscape orientation. If you make any page setup changes, save the worksheet again.
g. Display and print the worksheet formulas, then print the formulas on one page with row and column headings.
h. Close the workbook without saving the changes for displaying formulas, then exit Excel.

▶ Independent Challenge 2

You are an auditor with a certified public accounting firm. Fly Away, a manufacturer of skating products, has contacted you to audit its financial records. The management at Fly Away is considering opening a branch in Great Britain and needs its records audited to prepare the business plan. The managers at Fly Away have asked you to assist them in preparing their year-end sales summary as part of this audit. Specifically, they want to add expenses and show the percent of annual expenses that each expense category represents. They also want to show what percent of annual sales each expense category represents. You should include a formula calculating the difference between sales and expenses and another formula calculating expenses divided by sales. The expense categories and their respective dollar amounts are as follows: Building Lease $46,000; Equipment $208,000; Office $25,000; Salary $355,000; Taxes $310,000. Use these expense amounts to prepare the year-end sales and expenses summary for Fly Away.

a. Start Excel, open the Project File EX E-4 from the drive and folder where your Project Files are stored, then save the workbook as **Fly Away Sales**.
b. Name the cell containing the formula for total annual expenses **Annual_Expenses**. Use the name Annual_Expenses in cell C12 to create a formula calculating percent of annual expenses. Copy this formula as appropriate and apply the Percent style. Make sure to include a formula that sums all the values for percent of annual expenses, which should equal 100%.

c. Enter a formula calculating the percent of annual sales each expense category represents. Use the name **Annual_Sales** in the formula and format it appropriately. Copy this formula as appropriate and apply the Percent style. Make sure to include a formula that sums all the values for percent of annual sales.

d. Enter the formula calculating Net Profit, using the names Annual_Sales and Annual_Expenses.

e. Enter the formula for Expenses as a percent of sales, using the names Annual_Sales and Annual_Expenses.

f. Format the cells using the Currency, Percent, or Comma style as appropriate. Widen the columns as necessary to display cell contents.

g. Set the top and bottom margins at 4 inches and center the worksheet horizontally so the worksheet will print on two pages. *(Hint:* Use the Margins tab on the Page Setup dialog box.)

h. Print the first row containing the company name on each page. (*Hint*: Use the Sheet tab on the Page Setup dialog box and specify row 1 to repeat at the top.)

i. Enter your name into cell A22, then save, preview, and print the worksheet. Save any page setup changes you make.

j. Close the workbook then exit Excel.

► Independent Challenge 3

As the owner of Custom Fit, a general contracting firm specializing in home-storage projects, you are facing yet another business challenge at your firm. Because jobs are taking longer than expected, you decide to take out a loan to purchase some new power tools. According to your estimates, you need a $7,000 loan to purchase the tools. You check three loan sources: the Small Business Administration (SBA), your local bank, and a consortium of investors. The SBA will lend you the money at 8% interest, but you have to pay it off in three years. The local bank offers you the loan at 8.75% interest over four years. The consortium offers you a 7.75% loan, but they require you to pay it back in two years. To analyze all three loan options, you decide to build a tool loan summary worksheet. Using the loan terms provided, build a worksheet summarizing your options.

a. Start Excel, open a new workbook, then save it as **Custom Fit Loan Options** in the drive and folder where your Project Files are stored.

b. Enter today's date in cell A3, using the TODAY function.

c. Enter labels and worksheet data. You need headings for the loan source, loan amount, interest rate, term or number of payments, monthly payment, total payments, and total interest. Fill in the data provided for the three loan sources.

d. Enter formulas as appropriate: a PMT formula for the monthly payment, a formula calculating the total payments based on the monthly payment and term values, and a formula for total interest based on the total payments and the loan amount.

e. Format the worksheet as desired.

f. Enter your name in cell A14, then save, preview, and print the worksheet on a single page using landscape orientation. Print the worksheet formulas showing row and column headings. Do not save the worksheet with the formula settings.

g. Close the workbook then exit Excel.

Independent Challenge 4

The MediaLoft management wants to start IRAs for its employees. The company plans to deposit $2,000 in the employees' accounts at the beginning of each year. You have been asked to research current rates at financial institutions. You will use the Web to find this information.

a. Go to the Alta Vista search engine at www.altavista.com and enter "IRA rates" in the Search box. You can also use Yahoo, Excite, Infoseek or another search engine of your choice. Find IRA rates offered by three institutions for a $2,000 deposit, then write down the institution name, the rate, and the minimum deposit in the table below.

b. Start Excel, open a new workbook, then save it as **IRA Rates** in the drive and folder where your Project Files are stored.

c. Enter the column headings, row headings, and, research results from the table below into your IRA Rates workbook.

IRA WORKSHEET

Institution	Rate	Minimum Deposit	Number of Years	Amount Deposited (Yearly)	Future Value
			35	2000	
			35	2000	
			35	2000	
Highest Rate					
Average Rate					
Highest Future Value					

d. Use the FV function to calculate the future value of a $2,000 yearly deposit over 35 years for each institution, making sure it displays as a positive number. Assume that the payments are made at the beginning of the period, so the Type argument equals 1.

e. Use Excel functions to enter the highest rate, the average rate, and the highest future value into the workbook.

f. Enter your name in cell A15, then save, preview, and print the worksheet on a single page.

g. Display and print the formulas for the worksheet on a single page using landscape orientation. Do not save the worksheet with the formulas displayed.

h. Close the workbook then exit Excel.

▶ Visual Workshop

Create the worksheet shown in Figure E-22. (Hint: Enter the items in range C9:C11 as labels by typing an apostrophe before each formula.) Enter your name in row 15, and save the workbook as **Car Payment Calculator**. Preview, then print, the worksheet.

FIGURE E-22

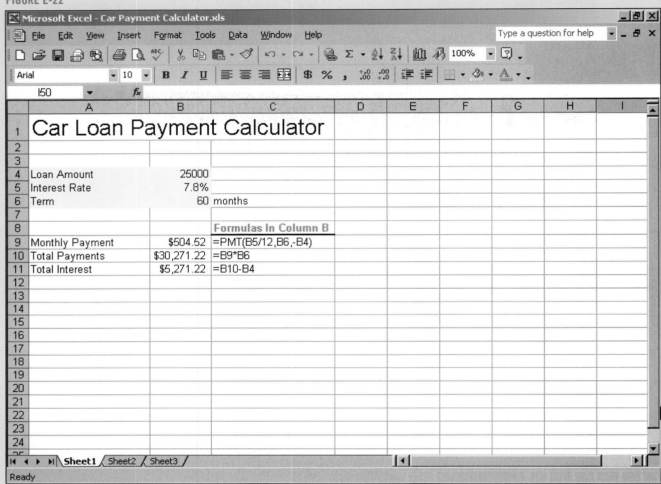

Project Files List

Read the following information carefully!

It is very important to organize and keep track of the files you need for this book.

1. Extract the files from the disk in the back of the book.

Please note that the Project Files have been compressed into a WinZip self-extracting executable file on the disk. To uncompress these files, complete the following steps:

- Insert the disk from the book into your computer, then locate the file **4530-2.EXE** in Windows Explorer or File Manager.

- Double-click the **.EXE** file. The WinZip Self-Extractor will open.

- To uncompress the files to the default directory of C:\4530-2, click **Unzip**. If you plan to store your work on floppy disks, extract the files to the C:\4530-2 directory.

- If you are storing your files in a location other than the default directory or on floppy disks, type the directory name in the Unzip to Folder text box.

- When the WinZip dialog box appears showing how many files have unzipped successfully, click **OK**, then click **Close**. The files will be organized according to unit.

2. Organize your Project Files onto disks, if you are using disks to store your work.

- In Windows Explorer, navigate to the C:\4530-2 folder.

- Make sure you copy all extracted files from the C:\4530-2 folder onto floppy disks, using the Project Files List or ReadMe file as a guide.

- Unless noted in the Project Files List, you will need one formatted, high-density disk for each unit. For each unit you plan to complete, copy the files listed in the **Project Files Supplied Column** onto one disk.

- Make sure you label each disk clearly with the unit name (e.g. Excel Unit A). Once you have created all your Project Disks, delete the C:\4530-2 folder.

3. Find and keep track of your Project Files and completed files.

- Use the **Project File Supplied column** to make sure you have the files you need before starting the unit or exercise indicated in the **Unit and Location column**.

- Use the **Student Saves File As column** to find out the filename you use when saving your changes to a Project File that was provided.

- Use the **Student Creates File column** to find out the filename you use when saving a file you create new for the exercise.

Unit and Location	Project File Supplied	Student Saves File As	Student Creates File
Excel Unit A			
Lessons	EX A-1.xls	MediaLoft Cafe Budget.xls	
Skills Review	EX A-2.xls	MediaLoft Toronto Cafe.xls	MediaLoft Balance Sheet.xls
Independent Challenge 1	(No files provided or created)		
Independent Challenge 2			Sample Payroll.xls
Independent Challenge 3			Training Workbook.xls
			Template Sample.xls
Independent Challenge 4			New Computer Data.xls
Visual Workshop			Carrie's Camera and Darkroom.xls
Excel Unit B			
Lessons	EX B-1.xls	Author Events Forecast.xls	
Skills Review	EX B-2.xls	Office Furnishings.xls	
Independent Challenge 1			Young Brazilians.xls
Independent Challenge 2	EX B-3.xls	Beautiful You Finances.xls	
Independent Challenge 3			Learn-it-All.xls
Independent Challenge 4			Temperature Conversions.xls
Visual Workshop			Annual Budget.xls
Excel Unit C			
Lessons	EX C-1.xls	Ad Expenses.xls	
Skills Review			MediaLoft GB Inventory.xls
	EX C-2.xls	Monthly Operating Expenses.xls	
Independent Challenge 1	EX C-3.xls	BY Inventory.xls	
Independent Challenge 2	EX C-4.xls	Community Action.xls	
Independent Challenge 3			Classic Instruments.xls
Independent Challenge 4			Currency Conversions.xls
Visual Workshop	EX C-5.xls	Projected March Advertising Invoices.xls	
Excel Unit D			
Lessons	EX D-1.xls	MediaLoft Sales - Eastern Division.xls	
Skills Review			MediaLoft Vancouver Software Usage.xls
Independent Challenge 1	EX D-2.xls	Springfield Theater Group.xls	
Independent Challenge 2	EX D-3.xls	BY Expense Charts.xls	
Independent Challenge 3	EX D-4.xls	Bright Light.xls	
Independent Challenge 4			New Location Analysis.xls
Visual Workshop	EX D-5.xls	Quarterly Advertising Budget.xls	

Unit and Location	Project File Supplied	Student Saves File As	Student Creates File
Excel Unit E			
Lessons	EX E-1.xls	Company Data.xls	
Skills Review	EX E-2.xls	Manager Bonuses.xls	
Independent Challenge 1	EX E-3.xls	Mike's Sales.xls	
Independent Challenge 2	EX E-4.xls	Fly Away Sales.xls	
Independent Challenge 3			Custom Fit Loan Options.xls
Independent Challenge 4			IRA Rates.xls
Visual Workshop			Car Payment Calculator.xls

Microsoft Excel 2002 MOUS Certification Objectives

Below is a list of the Microsoft Office User Specialist program objectives for the Core Excel 2002 skills, showing where each MOUS objective is covered in the Lessons and Practice. This table lists the Core MOUS certification skills covered in the units in this book (Units A-E). The core skills without page references are covered in *Microsoft Excel – 2002 Illustrated Intermediate*. For more information on which Illustrated titles meet MOUS certification, please see the inside cover of this book.

MOUS standardized coding number	Activity	Lesson page where skill is covered	Location in lesson where skill is covered	Practice
Ex2002-1	**Working with Cells and Cell Data**			
Ex2002-1-1	Insert, delete and move cells	EXCEL B-12	Step 7	Skills Review
		EXCEL B-19	Clues to Use	Skills Review
		EXCEL C-6	Step 6	Skills Review, Independent Challenge 4
Ex2002-1-2	Enter and edit cell data including text, numbers, and formulas	EXCEL A-10	Steps 1-7 Step 2 Tip	Skills Review, Independent Challenges 2-4
		EXCEL B-4	Steps 2-9	Skills Review
		EXCEL B-6	Steps 1-6	Skills Review, Independent Challenges 1-4
		EXCEL B-8	Steps 1-5, Clues to Use	Skills Review, Independent Challenges 1-4
		EXCEL B-10	Steps 2-9	Skills Review, Independent Challenge 2
		EXCEL C-2	Steps 2-7	Skills Review, Independent Challenges 1-4
		EXCEL C-3	Clues to Use	Skills Review, Independent Challenges 1-4
		EXCEL E-2	Steps 3-5	Skills Review, Independent Challenges 1, 3, 4
		EXCEL E-8	Steps 1-3	Skills Review, Independent Challenges 1, 3
Ex2002-1-3	Check spelling	EXCEL C-16	Steps 1-5	Skills Review, Independent Challenges 1-4
Ex2002-1-4	Find and replace cell data and formats	EXCEL E-2	Step 2	Skills Review
Ex2002-1-5	Work with a subset of data by filtering lists			
Ex2002-2	**Managing Workbooks**			
Ex2002-2-1	Manage workbook files and folders	EXCEL A-8	Steps 1-3, Step 4 Tip	Skills Review
Ex2002-2-2	Create workbooks using templates	EXCEL A-9	Clues to Use	Independent Challenge 3
Ex2002-2-3	Save workbooks using different names and file formats	EXCEL A-8	Step 4 Tip	Skills Review
		EXCEL A-8	Steps 4-5	Skills Review, Independent Challenges 1-4
		EXCEL C-2	Step 1 Tip	Skills Review, Independent Challenges 3-4
Ex2002-3	**Formatting and Printing Worksheets**			
Ex2002-3-1	Apply and modify cell formats	EXCEL C-2	Steps 2-7	Skills Review, Independent Challenges 1-4
		EXCEL C-3	Clues to Use	Skills Review
		EXCEL C-4	Steps 2-5	Skills Review, Independent Challenges 2, Visual Workshop
		EXCEL C-6	Steps 1-7	Skills Review, Independent Challenges 1-4, Visual Workshop
		EXCEL C-12	Steps 1-8	Skills Review, Independent Challenges 1, 2, 4, Visual Workshop

MOUS standardized coding number	Activity	Lesson page where skill is covered	Location in lesson where skill is covered	Practice
Ex2002-3-1		EXCEL C-14	Steps 2-5	Skills Review, Independent Challenge 1, 2, 4, Visual Workshop
Ex2002-3-2	Modify row and column settings	EXCEL C-10	Steps 1-6	Skills Review, Independent Challenges 1, 2
Ex2002-3-3	Modify row and column formats	EXCEL C-6 EXCEL C-7 EXCEL C-8 EXCEL C-9	Steps 6-7 Table Steps 1-7 Clues to Use	Skills Review, Independent Challenges 2-4 Skills Review, Independent Challenges 1-3 Independent Challenge 3
Ex2002-3-4	Apply styles	EXCEL E-4	Step 4	Skills Review, Independent Challenge 2
Ex2002-3-5	Use automated tools to format worksheets	EXCEL C-7	Clues to Use	Independent Challenges 3, 4
Ex2002-3-6	Modify Page Setup options	EXCEL C-16 EXCEL D-16 EXCEL E-16 EXCEL E-16 EXCEL E-17	Step 8 Step 4 Step 7 Tip Intro, Step 5 tip Step 6 Clues to Use	Independent Challenge 2 Skills Review, Independent Challenges 1-4 Independent Challenge 2 Skills Review, Independent Challenges 1, 3, 4 Independent Challenge 2
Ex2002-3-7	Preview and print worksheets and workbooks	EXCEL A-14	Steps 1-5	Skills Review, Independent Challenges 1-4
Ex2002-4	**Modifying Workbooks**			
Ex2002-4-1	Insert and delete worksheets			
Ex2002-4-2	Modify worksheet names and positions	EXCEL A-12 EXCEL A-12	Step 7 Steps 3-6 Step 3 Tip	Skills Review Skills Review, Independent Challenge 3
Ex2002-4-3	Use 3-D references			
Ex2002-5	**Creating and Revising Formulas**			
Ex2002-5-1	Create and revise formulas	EXCEL B-6 EXCEL B-8 EXCEL B-10 EXCEL B-14 EXCEL B-16 EXCEL B-18 EXCEL E-2 EXCEL E-12	Steps 1-6 Steps 1-5, Clues to Use Steps 1-4, 6 (Concept) Steps 1-6 Steps 4-7 Steps 2-5 Steps 1-3	Skills Review, Independent Challenges 1, 4, Visual Workshop Skills Review, Independent Challenges 1,4, Visual Workshop Independent Challenge 2 Skills Review Independent Challenges 1, 4 Skills Review, Independent Challenges 1, 4, Visual Workshop Skills Review, Independent Challenges 1, 4, Visual Workshop Skills Review Skills Review
Ex2002-5-2	Use statistical date and time, financial, and logical functions in formulas	EXCEL B-10 EXCEL B-11 EXCEL E-2 EXCEL E-8 EXCEL E-10 EXCEL E-12 EXCEL E-14 EXCEL E-15	Steps 1-4, 6 Clues to Use Steps 3-5 Steps 1-2 Steps 1-4 Steps 1-7 Steps 1-3 Clues to Use	Independent Challenge 2 Skills Review Skills Review Skills Review, Independent Challenge 1 Skills Review Skills Review, Independent Challenge 4 Skills Review, Independent Challenge 3, Visual Workshop Independent Challenge 4
Ex2002-6	**Creating and Modifying Graphics**			
Ex2002-6-1	Create, modify, position and print charts	EXCEL D-4 EXCEL D-8	Steps 2-7 Steps 3-6	Skills Review, Independent Challenges 1-4 Skills Review, Independent Challenges 1-4

MOUS standardized coding number	Activity	Lesson page where skill is covered	Location in lesson where skill is covered	Practice
		EXCEL D-10	Steps 1-6	Skills Review, Independent Challenges 1-4
		EXCEL D-12	Steps 1-8	Skills Review, Independent Challenges 1, 3
		EXCEL D-14	Steps 1-8	Skills Review, Independent Challenges 2, 3, Visual Workshop
		EXCEL D-16	Steps 2-7	Skills Review, Independent Challenges 1-4, Visual Workshop
		EXCEL D-17	Clues	Skills Review, Independent Challenge 1-4, Visual Workshop
Ex2002-6-2	Create, modify and position graphics	EXCEL C-5	Clues to Use	Independent Challenge 3
		EXCEL D-14	Steps 1-8	Skills Review, Independent Challenges 2, 3, Visual Workshop
Ex2002-7	**Workgroup Collaboration**			
Ex2002-7-1	Convert worksheets into web pages			
Ex2002-7-2	Create hyperlinks			
Ex2002-7-3	View and edit comments	EXCEL C-11	Clues to Use	Skills Review

Glossary

Excel 2002

3-D references A reference that uses values on other sheets or workbooks, effectively creating another dimension to a workbook.

Absolute reference A cell reference that contains a dollar sign before the column letter and/or row number to indicate the absolute, or fixed, contents of specific cells. For example, the formula $A$1+$B$1 calculates only the sum of these specific cells no matter where the formula is copied in the workbook.

Active cell The current location of the cell pointer.

Address See *Cell address*.

Alignment The placement of cell contents; for example, left, center, or right.

Area chart A line chart in which each area is given a solid color or pattern to emphasize the relationship between the pieces of charted information.

Arguments Information that a function needs to create an answer. In an expression, multiple arguments are separated by commas. All of the arguments are enclosed in parentheses; for example, =SUM(A1:B1).

Argument ToolTip A yellow box that appears as you build a function; shows function elements, which you can click to display online help for each one.

Arithmetic operator A symbol used in a formula (such as + or -, / or *) to perform mathematical operations.

Ask a Question box The list box at the right end of the menu bar in which you can type or select questions for the Help system.

Attribute The styling features such as bold, italics, and underlining that can be applied to cell contents.

AutoComplete A feature that automatically completes entries based on other entries in the same column.

AutoFill A feature that creates a series of text entries or numbers when a range is selected using the fill handle.

AutoFit A feature that automatically adjusts the width of a column to accommodate its widest entry when the boundary to the right of the column selector is double-clicked.

AutoFormat Preset schemes that can be applied to format a range instantly. Excel comes with 16 AutoFormats that include colors, fonts, and numeric formatting.

AutoSum A feature that automatically creates totals using the SUM function when you click the AutoSum button.

Background color The color applied to the background of a cell.

Bar chart A chart that shows information as a series of horizontal bars.

Border The edge of a cell, an area of a worksheet, or a selected object; you can change its color or line style.

Cancel button The X in the Formula bar; it removes information from the formula bar and restores the previous cell entry.

Cell The intersection of a column and row in a worksheet, datasheet, or table.

Cell address The location of a cell expressed by the column and row coordinates; the cell address of the cell in column A, row 1, is A1.

Cell pointer A highlighted rectangle around a cell that indicates the active cell.

Cell reference The address or name that identifies a cell's position in a worksheet; it consists of a letter that identifies the cell's column and a number that identifies its row; for example, cell B3. Cell references in worksheets can be used in formulas and are relative or absolute.

Chart A graphic representation of worksheet information. Types include 2-D and 3-D column, bar, pie, area, and line charts.

Chart sheet A separate sheet that contains only a chart linked to worksheet data.

Chart title The name assigned to a chart.

Chart Wizard A series of dialog boxes that helps you create or modify a chart.

Circular reference A formula that refers to its own cell location.

Clear A command on the Edit menu used to erase a cell's contents, formatting, or both.

Clipboard A temporary storage area for cut or copied items that are available for pasting. See *Office Clipboard*.

Clipboard task pane A task pane that shows the contents of the Office Clipboard; contains options for copying and pasting items.

Close A command that closes the file so you can no longer work with it, but keeps Excel open so that you can continue to work on other workbooks.

Column chart The default chart type in Excel, which displays information as a series of vertical columns.

Column heading The gray box containing the letter above the column.

Complex formula An equation that uses more than one type of arithmetic operator.

Conditional format A cell format that is based on the cell's value or the outcome of a formula.

Consolidate To combine values on multiple worksheets and show the result on another worksheet.

Control menu box A box in the upper-left corner of a window used to resize or close a window.

Copy A command that copies the selected cell's contents and places them on the Clipboard.

Cut A command that removes the cell contents from the selected area of a worksheet and places them on the Clipboard.

Database An organized collection of related information. In Excel, a database is called a list.

Data entry area The unlocked portion of a worksheet where users are able to enter and change data.

Data form In an Excel list (or database), a dialog box that displays one record at a time.

Data Marker A graphical representation of a data point, such as a bar or column.

Data point Individual piece of data plotted in a chart.

Data series The selected range in a worksheet that Excel converts into a graphic and displays as a chart.

Delete A command that removes cell contents from a worksheet.

Dialog box A window that opens when a program needs more information to carry out a command.

Dummy column/row Blank column or row included at the end of a range that enables a formula to adjust when columns or rows are added or deleted.

Dynamic page breaks In a larger workbook, horizontal or vertical dashed lines that represent the place where pages print separately. They also adjust automatically when you insert or delete rows or columns, or change column widths or row heights.

Edit A change made to the contents of a cell or worksheet.

Electronic spreadsheet A computer program that performs calculations on data and organizes information into worksheets. A worksheet is divided into columns and rows, which form individual cells.

Enter button The check mark in the formula bar used to confirm an entry.

Exploding pie slice A slice of a pie chart that has been pulled away from the whole pie to add emphasis.

External reference indicator The exclamation point (!) used in a formula to indicate that a referenced cell is outside the active sheet.

Field In a list (an Excel database), a column that describes a characteristic about records, such as first name or city.

Field name A column label that describes a field.

Fill color The cell background color.

Fill Down A command that duplicates the contents of the selected cells in the range selected below the cell pointer.

Fill handle A small square in the lower-right corner of the active cell used to copy cell contents.

Fill Right A command that duplicates the contents of the selected cells in the range selected to the right of the cell pointer.

Find A command used to locate information the user specifies.

Find & Replace A command used to find one set of information and replace it with new information.

Floating toolbar A toolbar within its own window, not anchored along an edge of the worksheet.

Font The typeface or design of a set of characters.

Font size The size of characters, measured in units called points (pts).

Footer Information that prints at the bottom of each printed page; on the screen, a footer is visible only in Print Preview. To add a footer, use the Header and Footer command on the View menu.

Format The appearance of text and numbers, including color, font, attributes, borders, and shading. See also *Number format*.

Format Painter A feature used to copy the formatting applied to one set of text or in one cell to another.

Formatting toolbar A toolbar that contains buttons for frequently used formatting commands.

Formula A set of instructions used to perform numeric calculations (adding, multiplying, averaging, etc.).

Formula bar The area below the menu bar and above the Excel workspace where you enter and edit data in a worksheet cell. The formula bar becomes active when you start typing or editing cell data. It includes the Enter button and the Cancel button.

Formula prefix An arithmetic symbol, such as the equal sign (=), used to start a formula.

Freeze To keep columns or rows in place so they remain visible while other parts of the worksheet are viewed.

Function A special, predefined formula that provides a shortcut for a commonly used calculation; for example, AVERAGE.

Function Wizard A feature that provides assistance in entering the arguments for a selected function.

Gridlines Horizontal and/or vertical lines within a chart that make the chart easier to read.

Header Information that prints at the top of each worksheet in a workbook. To add a header, use the Header and Footer command on the View menu.

Help system A utility that gives you immediate access to definitions, steps, explanations, and useful tips.

Hide To make rows, columns, formulas, or sheets invisible to workbook users.

Hyperlink Text or an object in a document that, when clicked, opens another document, worksheet or Web page.

Hypertext Markup Language (HTML) The language used to describe the content and format of Web pages.

Input Information that produces desired results, or output, in a worksheet.

Insertion point The blinking vertical line that appears in the formula bar or in a cell during editing in Excel.

Intranet An internal computer network that is used by a group of people, such as employees in a company's office.

Keyword A representative word on which the Help system can search to find information on your area of interest.

Label Descriptive text or other information that identifies the rows and columns of a worksheet. Labels are not included in calculations.

Label prefix A character, such as the apostrophe, that identifies an entry as a label and controls the way it appears in the cell.

Landscape orientation A print setting that positions the worksheet on the page so the page is wider than it is tall.

Legend A key explaining how information is represented by colors or patterns in a chart.

Line chart A graph of data that is mapped by a series of lines. Line charts show changes in data or categories of data over time and can be used to document trends.

Linking The dynamic referencing of data in other workbooks, so that when data in the other workbooks is changed, the references in the current workbook are automatically updated.

List The Excel term for a database, an organized collection of related information.

Lock To secure a row, column, or sheet so that data therein cannot be changed.

Logical test The first part of an IF function; if the logical test is true, then the second part of the function is applied, and if it is false, then the third part of the function is applied.In the function IF (Balance>1000, Balance*0.05,0), 5% of the balance is calculated if the balance exceeds $1,000.

Macro A set of instructions, or code, that performs tasks in the order you specify.

Menu bar The bar beneath the title bar that contains the names of menus, that when clicked, open menus from which you choose program commands.

Mixed reference A formula containing both a relative and absolute reference.

Mode indicator A box located at the lower-left corner of the status bar that informs you of a program's status. For example, when Excel is performing a task, the word "Wait" appears.

Module A program container attached to a workbook that holds a macro.

Mouse pointer A symbol that indicates the current location of the mouse on the desktop. The mouse pointer changes its shape to indicate what you can do next; for example, when you insert data, select a range, position a chart, change the size of a window or a column, or select a topic in Help.

Moving border The dashed line that appears around a cell or range that is copied to the Clipboard.

Name box The left-most area in the formula bar that shows the cell reference or name of the active cell. For example, A1 refers to cell A1 of the active worksheet. You can also display a list of names in a workbook using the Name list arrow.

Named range A range of cells given a meaningful name; it retains its name when moved and can be referenced in a formula.

New workbook task pane A task pane that lets you quickly open new or existing workbooks.

Number format A format applied to values to express numeric concepts, such as currency, date, and percentage.

Object A chart or graphic image that can be moved and resized and that contains handles when selected.

Office Assistant An animated character that appears to offer tips, answer questions, and provide access to a program's Help system.

Office Assistant tip A hint, indicated by the appearance of an onscreen light bulb, about the current action you are performing.

Office Clipboard A temporary storage area shared by all Office programs that can be used to cut, copy and paste multiple items within and between Office programs. The Office Clipboard can hold up to 24 items collected from any Office program. See also *Clipboard task pane.*

Open A command that retrieves a file from a disk and displays it on the screen.

Order of precedence The order in which Excel calculates parts of a formula: (1) exponents, (2) multiplication and division, and (3) addition and subtraction.

Output The end result of a worksheet.

Panes Sections into which you can divide a worksheet when you want to work on separate parts of the worksheet at the same time; one pane freezes, or remains in place, while you scroll in another pane until you see the desired information.

Paste A command that copies information on the Clipboard to a new location. Excel pastes the formula, rather than the result, unless the Paste Special command is used.

Paste Function A series of dialog boxes that helps you build functions; it lists and describes all Excel functions.

Paste Options Button A button that appears after an item is pasted; click its list arrow to keep source formatting, match destination cell formatting or keep the source cell's column widths.

Personal Macro Workbook A place to store commonly used macros that are available to all workbooks.

Pie chart A circular chart that represents data as slices of a pie. A pie chart is useful for showing the relationship of parts to a whole; pie slices can be extracted for emphasis. See also *Exploding pie slice.*

Plot area The area inside the horizontal and vertical chart axes.

Point A unit of measure used for fonts and row height. One inch equals 72 points, or a point is equal to $\frac{1}{72}$ of an inch.

Pointing method Specifying formula cell references by selecting the desired cell with the mouse instead of typing its cell reference; it eliminates typing errors. Also known as Pointing.

Portrait orientation A print setting that positions the worksheet on the page so the page is taller than it is wide.

Precedence Algebraic rules that Excel uses to determine the order of calculations in a formula with more than one operator.

Print Preview A command you can use to view a worksheet as it will look when printed. Also known as Previewing a worksheet.

Print title In a list that spans more than one page, the field names that print at the top of every printed page.

Program Task-oriented software (such as Excel) that enables you to perform a certain type of task, such as data calculation.

Program Code Program instructions used to create a macro.

Programs menu The Windows 95/98/ME/2000 Start menu that lists all available programs on your computer.

Publish Excel data Place a workbook or worksheet on a network or the Web.

Range A selected group of adjacent cells.

Range finder A feature that outlines an equation's arguments in blue and green.

Range format A format applied to a selected range in a worksheet.

Record In a list (an Excel database), data about an object or a person.

Replace A command used to find one set of criteria and replace it with new information.

Relative cell reference A type of cell reference used to indicate a relative position in the worksheet. It allows you to copy and move formulas from one area to another of the same dimensions. Excel automatically changes the column and row numbers to reflect the new position. Also known as Relative reference.

Row height The vertical dimension of a cell.

Row heading The gray box containing the row number to the left of the row.

Run a macro Test or execute a macro.

Save To store a file permanently on a disk or to overwrite the copy of a file that is stored on a disk with the changes made to the file.

Save As Command used to save a file for the first time or to create a new file with a different filename, leaving the original file intact.

Selection handles Small boxes appearing along the corners and sides of charts and graphic images that are used for moving and resizing.

Series of labels Preprogrammed series, such as days of the week and months of the year. They are formed by typing the first word of the series, then dragging the fill handle to the desired cell.

Sheet A term used for a worksheet.

Sheet tab A description at the bottom of each worksheet that identifies it in a workbook. In an open workbook, move to a worksheet by clicking its sheet tab. Also known as Worksheet tab.

Sheet tab scrolling buttons Buttons that enable you to move among sheets within a workbook.

Sort keys Criteria on which a sort, or a reordering of data, is based.

Spelling check A command that attempts to match all text in a worksheet with the words in the dictionary.

Standard toolbar A toolbar that contains buttons for frequently used operating and editing commands.

Start To open a software program so you can use it.

Status bar The bar at the bottom of the Excel window that provides information about various keys, commands, and processes.

Style A combination of formatting characteristics.

SUM The most frequently used function, this adds columns or rows of cells.

Target The file that a hyperlink displays when you click it.

Task pane A window area to the right of the worksheet that provides worksheet options, such as creating a new workbook, conducting a search, inserting Clip Art, and using the Office Clipboard.

Template An Excel file saved with a special format that lets you open a new file based on an existing workbook's design and/or content.

Text annotations Labels added to a chart to draw attention to a particular area.

Text color The color applied to text in a cell or on a chart.

Tick marks Notations of a scale of measure on a chart axis.

Title bar The bar at the top of the program window that indicates the program name and the name of the current file.

Toggle button A button that turns a feature on and off.

Toolbar A bar that contains buttons that you can click to perform commands.

Toolbar Options button A button you click on a toolbar to view toolbar buttons not currently visible.

Truncate To shorten the display of cell information because a cell is too wide.

Values Numbers, formulas, or functions used in calculations.

Value axis Also known as the y-axis in a 2-dimensional chart, this area often contains numerical values that help you interpret the size of chart elements.

View A set of display and/or print settings that you can name and save for access at another time. You can save multiple views of a worksheet.

What-if analysis A decision-making feature in which data is changed and formulas based on it are automatically recalculated.

Wildcard Character A special symbol you use in defining search criteria in the data form or Replace dialog box. The most common types of wildcards are the question mark (?), which stands for any single character, and the asterisk (*), which represents any group of characters.

Window A rectangular area of a screen where you view and work on the open file.

Workbook A collection of related worksheets contained within a single file.

Worksheet An electronic spreadsheet containing 256 columns by 65,536 rows.

Worksheet menu bar The toolbar at the top of the Excel screen.

Worksheet tab See *Sheet tab*.

Workspace A group of workbooks that can be opened in one step.

World Wide Web (Web) A structure of documents, called pages, connected by hyperlinks over a large computer network called the Internet.

X-axis The horizontal axis in a chart; because it often shows data categories, such as months, it is also called the category axis.

X-axis label A label describing a chart's x-axis.

Y-axis The vertical axis in a chart; because it often shows numerical values in a 2 dimensional chart, it is also called the value axis.

Y-axis label A label describing the y-axis of a chart.

Zoom A feature that enables you to focus on a larger or smaller part of the worksheet in Print Preview.

Index

Index